An Overview of the Public Relations Function

An Overview of the Public Relations Function

Shannon A. Bowen

Syracuse University

Brad Rawlins

Brigham Young University

Thomas Martin

College of Charleston

An Overview of the Public Relations Function

First published in 2010 by
Business Expert Press, LLC
222 East 46th Street, New York, NY 10017
www.businessexpertpress.com

ISBN-13: 978-1-60649-099-0 (paperback)
ISBN-10: 1-60649-099-0 (paperback)

ISBN-13: 978-1-60649-100-3 (e-book)
ISBN-10: 1-60649-100-8 (e-book)

DOI 10.4128/9781606491003.

A publication in the Business Expert Press Public Relations collection

Collection ISSN (print) forthcoming
Collection ISSN (electronic) forthcoming

Cover design by Jonathan Pennell
Interior design by Scribe, Inc.

First edition: April 2010

10 9 8 7 6 5 4 3 2 1

Printed in Taiwan

Abstract

This book provides an executive review of the field of public relations with a focus on what managers need to know in order to master the function quickly and effectively. Throughout the text, we integrate the academic with the professional by asking, how can an executive use this knowledge to make the most of the public relations function, department, and initiatives in order to help their whole organization be successful?

Part I of the book provides the busy manager with the taxonomy of the public relations field, provides research on the theory of public relations, and examines the structure of organizations and where public relations fits within that structure. Part II examines how public relations should be conducted in order to achieve maximum results and provides a comprehensive review of public relations strategy, including how to conduct a public relations campaign. Part III discusses the organizational settings most common in public relations: corporate, agency, government, or public affairs and nonprofit or advocacy groups and the public relations approaches common in each. We review what research finds regarding the most excellent ways to manage public relations and the best ways to analyze and address the ethical challenges to be faced in public relations. We occasionally use short case examples to illustrate and apply the main points managers will need to know in order to manage public relations effectively.

Throughout this book, we focus on the managerial pursuits in public relations, such as strategic relationship maintenance, segmentation of publics, and conducting research. We offer insight into the managerial activities of issues management, lobbying and advocacy, creating stakeholder relationships, reputation management, ethical counsel, and corporate communication. We examine the most current thought in public relations to help the busy manager master the most important concepts in the field quickly, accessibly, and with an eye toward helping an organization or client achieve the most effective results through cutting-edge, modern, research-based strategic public relations management.

Keywords

Strategic public relations management, reputation, organization-public relationships, corporate communication, ethics, excellence, issues management

Contents

Preface

Our purpose in this volume is to introduce you to the concepts of strategic public relations. Our basic assumption is that you have some general knowledge of management and business terminology; we will help you to apply that to the discipline of public relations. Our text is based in current research and scholarly knowledge of the public relations discipline as well as years of experience in professional public relations practice.

Whether you are reading this book to learn a new field, simply to update your knowledge, or as part of an educational program or course, we value every moment that you spend with it. Therefore, we have eliminated much of the academic jargon found in other books and used a straightforward writing style. We tried to make the chapters short enough to be manageable, but packed with information, without an overreliance on complicated examples or charts and diagrams. We hope that our no-nonsense approach will speed your study.

We use a few original public relations case studies that we have written for you so that you can see the concepts we discuss illustrated and applied. This book is divided into three large parts:

- *Part I: Mastering the Basics.* Chapters 1 through 4 focus on the importance of the profession, its taxonomy, the academic research showing how public relations should be conducted, and the function as a part of management.
- *Part II: Organizations and Processes.* Chapters 5 through 9 offer a look at organization, its structure, effectiveness, and how the public relations process is managed—through the relationships with publics and stakeholders, conducting research, and the process of strategically managing public relations.
- *Part III: The Practice and Best Practices.* Chapters 10 through 12 provide an advanced discussion of public relations specialties by types: corporations, agencies, government and public affairs units, nonprofits, NGOs, and activist groups. We offer

guidance for perhaps the most difficult situations in public relations—counseling upon ethics and taking a leadership role—and finally we discuss what research shows regarding how to make the public relations function the best it can be.

We recommend reading the book in this order to build upon the logical flow of terminology, processes, and management knowledge. Here is a closer look at what we discuss.

To introduce the critical function of public relations to an organization and to show how public relations can work to prevent issues and crises, we begin with a case study of United Parcel Service in Chapter 1. Then we emphasize what was learned in this case from the failure of public relations in order to prepare in advance for any contingency. In Chapter 2, we introduce the taxonomy of the profession and the concepts prevalent in the strategic management of relationships with publics, and introduce some different names associated with this function. Chapter 3 is an exceptionally important chapter because it introduces the models and approaches to public relations that provide a taxonomy for evaluating communications efforts. The models of public relations are introduced through a brief history of the field, and we also examine the subfunctions or specialties within the profession. Numerous key definitions are provided to help you rapidly master the lexicon of public relations and its professional practice.

Chapter 4 discusses the inclusion of public relations as a management function, roles and access to the C-suite, decision making, and the core competencies for working in business, including knowledge of strategy and profit motivations. We discuss how chief communications officers (CCOs) earn their seat at the executive table. Much real-world professional experience in business settings provide the backbone of the chapter. Chapter 5 is extremely important because it discusses how public relations should be organized and structured, and how it should "fit" within the larger organizational culture in order to provide it with the maximum opportunity for success. The chapter draws on research from public relations scholars, business management scholars, and organizational theory. Chapter 6 provides an in-depth discussion of how organizations define success, and how the stakeholder management approach to public relations can provide a concrete strategy for enhancing organizational effectiveness and can contribute to the long-term sustainability of organizations.

How strategic public relations is practiced is covered in Chapter 7. Strategic public relations begins with identifying and prioritizing your publics, and building ongoing relationships with them, based on the advanced concepts of stakeholder management. Research is an essential element in strategic public relations and an overview of those methods is provided in Chapter 8, as well as an explanation of the importance of research in strategy and in management. Chapter 9 gives an overview of the four-step process of strategic public relations management, abbreviated as RACE, and associated processes of analysis and planning.

The more advanced discussions of public relations as a strategic management function begins with Chapter 10. It provides a detailed look at the profession by highlighting the locales in which it is practiced, and it offers a discussion and application of the concepts presented earlier throughout this text. We attempt to integrate these theoretical concepts into the real-life structure of day-to-day public relations, and include a couple of case examples for illustration. Chapter 11 establishes the ethical and moral guidelines for practicing principled public relations that enhance the social responsibility of organizations and allows public relations managers to take leadership roles in advising the top levels of their organizations. We follow that discussion with a look inside the top level of the Home Depot Corporation. Finally, Chapter 12 sums up the book by illustrating the best practices for excellent public relations. That summary of current research will reinforce your understanding of the lexicon of modern public relations management, how research says that it can be practiced most effectively, and the importance to an organization of strategic communication. That importance can be seen in the Entergy/Hurricane Katrina case that concludes our book.

We hope that you enjoy this executive text as we seek to help you master the dynamic field that is strategic relationship creation and maintenance through communication management.

PART I

Mastering the Basics

CHAPTER 1

The Importance of Public Relations

Case: UPS Faces Losses in Teamster's Union Strike[1]

Public relations can truly mean the difference between life and death for an organization, or the difference between profitability and failure. The following case illustrates the importance of public relations as a means to maintain ongoing, beneficial relationships, to systematically listen to and understand the concerns of publics—in this case, internal publics and a labor union and the external public of news media. Ongoing public relations initiatives, such as strategic issues management, could have prevented the problems encountered by the organization in the following case. The case also demonstrates that an organization can recover its footing and repair its reputation and relationships, once it acknowledges its mistakes and commits to changing course. The following series of events highlight the importance of ongoing, strategic public relations as the very lifeblood of an organization.

A Conflict Unfolds

United Parcel Service (UPS), the world's largest transportation and logistics company, faced a difficult set of challenges as the year 1997 began. The company, founded in 1907, plays a vital role in both the U.S. and global economy. UPS serves more than 200 countries and territories and delivered more than 3.8 billion packages—15 million packages a day—in 2008. The company achieved $51.5 billion in 2008 revenues and has more than eight million customer contacts per day. It is the second largest employer in the United States and the ninth largest in the world with 427,000 employees. UPS carries approximately 6% of U.S. gross domestic product (GDP) and 2% of global GDP.

UPS had a long and, for the most part, positive relationship with the International Brotherhood of Teamsters, the union that has represented UPS employees since the 1920s. In 1997, that relationship would be severely tested and the resulting impact on the company would be profound.

Negotiations with the Teamsters began in early January of that year, even though the existing contract didn't expire until 12:01 a.m. on August 1, 1997. UPS negotiates a national contract with the union every 4 to 6 years, and prior to 1997 there had never been a national strike by the union against UPS. The company is the largest employer of Teamsters in the country, with 225,000 members.

The president of the Teamsters was Ron Carey, a former UPS driver from New York City, who—according to many accounts—had left the company with a profound dislike for UPS. Carey had won reelection as president of the Teamsters in 1996, an election that later resulted in an investigation based on allegations of illegal fund-raising and kickbacks. As negotiations with the Teamsters began, Carey's opponents within the union were attacking him, seeking to erode his support and petitioning for possible new elections. Many believed there was a high likelihood that the federal investigation would result in Carey's election being overturned. Although UPS was not aware of it as negotiations began, Carey had been quietly preparing the union for a strike. He needed to make a show of force and leadership to galvanize his support in anticipation of rerunning for the presidency if the election was nullified.

At the start of negotiations the primary issues focused on traditional areas such as wages and health and retirement benefits. But two other areas proved to be far more important, especially in the communication battle that developed as negotiations began to break down. One of these was job security. UPS had utilized part-time employees for many years, and the Teamsters wanted the company to commit to the creation of a higher percentage of full-time jobs, with a guaranteed minimum number of these jobs.

A second underlying issue that heavily influenced the negotiations was control of the pensions for UPS employees in the union. At the time negotiations began, the Teamsters union controlled the pension fund, one of the largest funds in the United States. UPS questioned how the fund was being managed, the future pension security of its employees, and wanted a separate pension fund for its employees who were Teamsters.

As the negotiations began to deteriorate, the company began planning contingencies at all levels, including public relations. In 1997, UPS was still a privately held company. The public relations department was small, with only 10 management employees and a limited budget of $5 million in the United States. There were few trained spokespeople, since the company did not have the public disclosure obligations typical of publicly traded firms. The public relations department functions included product publicity, financial communications, reputation management, and executive communications through a speaker's bureau. The function was also responsible for overall message development, crisis management, sponsorships, and event support. But it was understaffed and underfunded to deal effectively with the global attention UPS was about to face.

The contract negotiations continued to unravel throughout the summer of 1997 and culminated with the Teamsters rejecting UPS's final contract offer on July 30. At that point, federal mediators intervened and continued negotiations through August 3. As the talks concluded at the end of the day, the union indicated it would return to the table the next day.

Without any forewarning, the Teamsters union announced to its members that evening that it would strike. Ron Carey held a press conference early in the morning on August 4 confirming a national strike and encouraging all UPS workers to walk out. The Teamsters had been developing a full-court media blitz, which they launched that day with a well-coordinated campaign using television, radio, and print.

The UPS strike instantly became the top national and local news story throughout the United States. The strike affected operations in more than 1,800 locations in all 50 states and generated media interest in every large- to medium-sized city. The UPS public relations office received more than 20,000 phone calls during the strike. According to Ken Sternad, who headed the function at the time, "We got slaughtered in the press."

The strike lasted 15 days and had a severe impact on U.S. and global commerce, costing UPS $750 million in lost revenue and related expenses. In the view of Sternad, the Teamsters won the communication battle largely because they had "key messages that played well."

"They focused their messaging around the theme of 'Part-time America won't work' and that caught on with the media," said Sternad. "The Teamsters had clearly tested and researched this message and the others they used. They communicated early and often, including holding twice-daily press briefings in Washington, DC. The Teamsters stayed in control of the message and it worked for them."

Sternad also pointed to the way in which the union put a human face on the issue by showcasing unhappy UPS workers, especially those with part-time employment. They effectively engaged third-party experts and made effective use of the Internet.

During the strike, UPS established a clear set of guiding principles and never wavered from these. The company's number one objective was to get a good contract; winning the public relations battle was not an objective. "We had decided early on that we would not attack the union leadership and not make our people a target," remembers Sternad. He continued,

> We knew that we would need our people with us for the long term and we didn't want to do or say anything that would tarnish the image of the UPS driver. They will always be the face of the company and our link to our customers and we didn't want to alienate them.

In preparing for the strike, UPS did have a formal crisis communications plan in place and they had developed a specific communications plan in the event of a strike. The public relations team had compiled extensive facts and figures about the company and had trained regional spokespeople in advance of a strike. They had also identified third-party experts who could point out the many positives of the company.

In retrospect, the company acknowledges that they could have done a better job of handling the communication before and during the strike. Says Sternad,

> We had essentially no communications in the first 24 hours. Our messages simply didn't resonate with the media or the general public, including our customers. We realized that we had not

> adequately tested our messages before or during the crisis. And we were much slower to utilize the web than the Teamsters. In the end we just didn't have the proper resources aligned to manage the crisis.

UPS learned valuable lessons from the experience that have served them well in preparing for future crises. Sternad notes,

> The real work begins before the crisis hits. The PR team must make decisions for the long-term and stay focused on priorities. As in all crises, the first hours are the most critical. How the company responds initially sets the tone for the rest of the crisis period. That is why advance research is so critical. Message testing is fundamental to effective communications, but it must be done before the crisis hits.
>
> We also saw clearly that in your messages you need steak *and* sizzle, facts along with powerful images that touch people's emotions, not just their intellect. We now cultivate and use third parties on an ongoing basis so that we know them and they know us long before a crisis. We maintain standby web sites that can be turned on instantly in the event of a crisis. As painful as it was at the time, I think we're a much stronger and better prepared company because of this experience.

Though UPS may have failed to gets its point across in the heat of the 1997 battle, the longer term story turned out differently. After the strike was settled, Teamsters president Ron Carey was removed from office, expelled from the union, and banned from participating in labor activities for life as a result of his involvement with election irregularities.

The Teamsters had retained control of the pension plan after the 1997 strike, but its financial health continued to erode in the years that followed. Pension benefits were cut, the retirement age was raised, and UPS ultimately negotiated a separate pension plan for more than 40,000 of its Teamster employees previously in the union plan. It cost UPS more than $6 billion to exit the union plan and cover its liabilities, compared to a fraction of that amount it would have cost if they had been granted control in 1997.

Following the resolution of the strike, UPS saw its strongest growth and most profitable years in 1998 and 1999. In 1999, UPS became a publicly traded company through the largest initial public offering of its stock in the history of Wall Street.

A year later, UPS was named by *Forbes* magazine as its "Company of the Year."

What Can Be Learned From the UPS Case?

Although UPS ultimately overcame the setbacks it incurred from the Teamsters strike of 1997, the company would have much preferred avoiding the strike altogether. Clearly, the strike had an adverse impact on the company's reputation, an impact that took years to reverse. The case demonstrates the importance of developing and maintaining relationships, even with those whom you may feel are adversaries. In this case, the company underestimated the Teamsters willingness to call for a strike. They also miscalculated the underlying resentment of Teamsters members toward the company. Once the strike was under way, the company began to regain its footing. Management consciously chose not to vilify its employees, even though they had walked off the job. This strategy proved to be a key in limiting the long-term damage from the strike and allowing UPS to recover its reputation and rebuild labor relations within a relatively short time.

CHAPTER 2

What Is Public Relations?

Public relations is a conduit, a facilitator, and a manager of communication, conducting research, defining problems, and creating meaning by fostering communication among many groups in society. The United Parcel Service (UPS) case illustrated the importance of this communication, both in financial terms—the strike cost UPS about $750 million—and in terms of reputation with strategic publics.

Public relations is a strategic conversation. As you might imagine, it is an ephemeral and wide-ranging field, often misperceived, and because of the lack of message control inherent in public relations, it is difficult to master. Public relations is even difficult to define. Is it spin or truth telling? Either way, the public relations function is prevalent and growing; the fragmentation of media and growth of multiple message sources means that public relations is on the ascent while traditional forms of mass communication (such as newspapers) are on the decline.

You can find public relations in virtually every industry, government, and nonprofit organization. Its broad scope makes it impossible to understand without some attention to the taxonomy of this diverse and dynamic profession. Learning the lexicon of public relations in this chapter will help you master the discipline and help your study move quicker in subsequent reading.

Corporate and agency public relations differ. These concepts are discussed in detail in a later chapter, along with nonprofit public relations and government relations or public affairs. For the purposes of an overview, we can define **corporate public relations** as being an in-house public relations department within a for-profit organization of any size. On the other hand, **public relations agencies** are hired consultants that normally work on an hourly basis for specific campaigns or goals of the organization that hires them. It is not uncommon for a large corporation to have both an in-house corporate public relations department and an external public relations agency that consults on specific issues. As their names imply, **nonprofit public relations** refers to not-for-profit organizations, foundations, and other issue- or cause-related groups. **Government relations** or **public affairs** is the branch of public relations that specializes in managing relationships with governmental officials and regulatory agencies.

Defining Public Relations

Among the many competing definitions of public relations, J. Grunig and Hunt's is the most widely cited definition of public relations: Public relations is "the *management of communication between an organization and its publics*."[1] One reason this definition is so successful is its parsimony, or using few words to convey much information. It also lays down the foundation of the profession squarely within management, as opposed to the competing approaches of journalism or the promotion-based approach of marketing and advertising that focuses primarily on consumers. The component parts of Grunig and Hunt's famous definition of public relations are as follows:

- **Management**. The body of knowledge on how best to coordinate the activities of an enterprise to achieve effectiveness.
- **Communication**. Not only sending a message to a receiver but also understanding the messages of others through listening and dialogue.
- **Organization**. Any group organized with a common purpose; in most cases, it is a business, a corporation, a governmental agency, or a nonprofit group.
- **Publics**. Any group(s) of people held together by a common interest. They differ from audiences in that they often self-organize and do not have to attune to messages; publics differ from stakeholders in that they do not necessarily have a financial stake tying them to specific goals or consequences of the organization. Targeted audiences, on the other hand, are publics who receive a specifically targeted message that is tailored to their interests.

As "the management of communication between an organization and its publics," public relations has radically departed from its historical roots in publicity and journalism to become a management discipline—that is, one based on research and strategy.

The Function of Public Relations

In 1982, the Public Relations Society of America (PRSA) adopted the following definition of public relations that helps identify its purpose: "Public relations helps an organization and its publics adapt mutually to each other."[2] In its "Official Statement on Public Relations," PRSA goes on to clarify the function of public relations:

- Public relations helps our complex, pluralistic society to reach decisions and function more effectively by contributing to mutual understanding among groups and institutions. It serves to bring private and public policies into harmony.
- Public relations serves a wide variety of institutions in society such as businesses, trade unions, government agencies, voluntary associations, foundations, hospitals, schools, colleges and religious institutions. To achieve their goals, these institutions must develop effective relationships with many different audiences or publics such as employees, members, customers, local communities, shareholders and other institutions, and with society at large.
- The managements of institutions need to understand the attitudes and values of their publics in order to achieve institutional goals. The goals themselves are shaped by the external environment. The public relations practitioner acts as a counselor to management and as a mediator, helping to translate private aims into reasonable, publicly acceptable policy and action.[3]

As such, the public relations *field* has grown to encompass the building of important relationships between an organization and its key publics through its actions and its communication. This perspective defines the field as a management function and offers insight into the roles and responsibilities of public relations professionals. The PRSA definition, however, is not perfect: A main weakness of that definition is that it requires public relations "to bring private and public policies into harmony."[4] In reality, we know that the relationships an organization has with all of its publics cannot always be harmonious. Further, that definition obligates us to act in the best interest of both the organization and its publics, which could be logically impossible if those interests are diametrically opposed. A few examples would be class action litigation, boycotts, and oppositional research and lobbying; despite the negative nature of those relationships, they still require public relations management and communication.

The unique management function of public relations is critical to the success of any organization that engages people in its operation, whether they are shareholders, employees, or customers. Although many people think of publicity as the sole purpose of public relations, this text will help you understand that publicity is a subfunction of the overall purpose of public relations and should not be confused with the broader function.

Naming the Public Relations Function

A plethora of terms has come to be associated with modern-day public relations practice. Because of the disreputable beginnings of public relations that we will briefly discuss next, it is often the case that organizations will choose to name their public relations function by another moniker. These various terms create much confusion about the responsibilities of public relations versus overlapping or competing organizational functions. The term corporate communication is the most common synonym for public relations in practice today,[5] followed by marketing communication and public affairs. We view the term corporate communication as a synonym for public relations, although some scholars argue that corporate communication only applies to for-profit organizations. However, we view **corporate communication** as a *goal-oriented communication process that can be applied not only in the business world but also in the world of nonprofits and nongovernmental organizations,* *educational foundations, activist groups, faith-based organizations, and so on*. The term public relations often leads to confusion between the media relations function, public affairs, corporate communication, and marketing promotions, leading many organizations to prefer the term corporate communication.

We believe that the key component of effective public relations or corporate communication is an element of *strategy*. Many scholars prefer to use the phrase **strategic public relations** to differentiate it from the often misunderstood general term public relations, or "PR," which can be linked to manipulation or "spin" in the minds of lay publics. Strategic communication management, strategic public relations, and corporate communication are synonyms for the concept displayed in the preceding definitions. To scholars in the area, public relations is seen as the larger profession and an umbrella term, comprising many smaller subfunctions, such as media relations or public affairs or investor relations. The subfunctions of public relations will be delineated later in this chapter. Academics tend to use the term public relations, whereas professionals tend to prefer the term corporate communication. Do not be distracted by the name debate and the myriad of synonyms possible. Whatever name you prefer or encounter, a strong body of knowledge in the field, based on academic study and professional practice, has solidified the importance of the concepts supporting the strategic communication function that we will discuss in this text.

Chapter Summary

This chapter has provided an introduction to the purpose of public relations. Although the public relations function goes by many different names, it is essential to understand that it is a unique management function that contributes to an organization's success through its focus on developing and maintaining relationships with key publics. Those publics are generally employees, financial stakeholders or shareholders, communities, governments at many levels, and the media. It is also important not to confuse the overall purpose of public relations with its subfunctions, such as publicity and media relations. These subfunctions will be defined in the next chapter and covered in more detail in Chapter 10.

CHAPTER 3

Models and Approaches to Public Relations

Although there were ancient public relations—as far in the past as ancient Greece—modern-day public relations in the United States began with a group of revolutionaries mounting a public relations campaign to turn public opinion in favor of independence from England and King George. The revolutionaries effectively used words and actions to mount a successful activist campaign leading to the Revolutionary War. Thomas Paine's *Common Sense*, published in 1776, gave rise to the sentiment that England's governance under King George III was unjust. The subsequent *Declaration of Independence* and outward acts of protest were largely influenced by the rhetorical arguments found in Paine's pamphlet, which has been called the most influential tract of the American Revolution. Slogans, such as *Don't Tread on Me*, and use of printed materials, such as Colonial newspapers, were key message tactics used to sway opinion in favor of a revolution and a war for independence. Following the independence, *The Federalist Papers* were used to ratify the United States Constitution. These 85 essays were, according to the assessment of Grunig and Hunt, exemplary forms of effective public relations.[1]

These founding fathers of the United States used public relations to build the public consensus necessary for a budding nation to form a new kind of government and establish the human rights necessary for the nation to survive.

The Historical Development of Modern Public Relations

Modern public relations in the United States can also be traced back to less illustrious beginnings than the creation of a new democratic republic.[2] P. T. Barnum, of circus fame, made his mark by originating and employing many publicity or press agentry tactics to generate attention for his shows and attractions. Barnum was famous for coining the phrase, "There's no such thing as bad publicity."[3] He was even known to pen letters to the editor under an assumed name outing some of his attractions as hoaxes just to generate publicity and keep a story alive. Unfortunately, Barnum's ethics left much to be desired.

One-Way Communication Models: Publicity and Dissemination of Information

Barnum thought that honesty was not the domain of a press agent, and infamously stated, "The public be fooled."[4] Droves of press agents followed in Barnum's tracks, in efforts to get free space in the news for their clients, ranging from Hollywood figures to private interests, such as railroads, and also politicians. This approach to public relations was termed **press agentry** by Grunig and Hunt because of its reliance on generating publicity with little regard for truth. For modern-day examples, we have to look only to the entertainment publicity surrounding a new film release, or the product publicity around a new energy drink or a new technological gadget. Publicity and press agentry are synonymous terms meaning simply to generate attention through the use of media.

The next historical phase resulted in a new model of public relations that Grunig and Hunt termed **public information**. In this approach to public relations, a former journalist works as a writer representing clients, issuing news releases to media outlets in the same style as journalistic writing. The idea of the public relations specialist acting as a counselor to management, as opposed to a simple practitioner of press agentry tactics, was born. The pioneering public information *counselor* was a man named Ivy Ledbetter Lee, who revolutionized public relations practice at the time with the idea of telling the truth. Lee studied at Harvard Law School, but went on to find a job as a journalist. After working as a successful journalist for a number of years, Ivy Lee realized that he had a real ability for explaining complicated topics to people, and had the idea of being a new kind of press agent. Rather than tricking the public, Lee saw his role as one of educating the public about truthful facts and supplying all possible information to the media. Ivy Lee opened the third public relations agency in the United States in 1904, representing clients such as the Pennsylvania Railroad, the Rockefeller family, and the Anthracite Coal Roads and Mine Company.[5] Lee became the first public relations practitioner to issue a code of ethics in 1906, based on his declaration that "the public be informed"—to replace railroad tycoon Commodore Cornelius Vanderbilt's infamous statement, "The public be damned."[6] Ivy Lee ushered in a more respectable form of public relations that is objective and factual. His public information approach is still in use today, especially in government reporting, quarterly earnings statements, and similar reports intended simply to inform.

Both the press agentry and public information models of public relations are based on writing and technical skill with images, words, Web sites, and media relations. These concepts are based on a one-way dissemination of information. They are not management-based models because strategic management is based on research. Research is what makes management a strategic pursuit based on knowledge and data that comprise two-way communication, as opposed to a simple one-way dissemination of information based on assumptions.

Two-Way Communication Models: Strategic Management of Public Relations

The next two models of public relations are based on research. Using research to gather public opinion data led scholars to label these models two-way rather than one-way because they more resemble a conversation than a simple dissemination of information. Grunig and Hunt termed the two management models *asymmetrical* and *symmetrical.*

The **asymmetrical model** was pioneered between 1920 and 1950 by Edward Bernays, nephew of psychoanalyst Sigmund Freud, and is based on the principles of behavioral psychology. Public relations research seeks to determine what publics know and understand or believe about the client organization, issues of importance, and so on. Then, in the asymmetrical model, once these beliefs are learned through polling and other means, they are incorporated into the public relations messages distributed by the organization. It is called asymmetrical because it is imbalanced in favor of the communicator; the communicator undergoes no real change, but simply uses the ideas she knows will resonate in communicating with publics with the purpose of persuading them on some issue or topic. For example, if I am a politician running for reelection and my research identifies tax cuts as an important topic with publics, then I include the importance of tax cuts in my next campaign speech. Research is a key component of this model, as it seeks to persuade publics to adopt the attitudes and beliefs that are favorable to the organization based on the collection of data about their existent beliefs.

The **symmetrical model** was also pioneered by Edward Bernays and several prominent public relations practitioners and educators between about 1960 to 1980. It seeks also to use research on public opinion just as the asymmetrical model does. However, it does not use research with the intent to persuade, but to build mutual understanding between both publics and organizations. Organizations are open to changing their internal policies and practices in this model based on what they learn from their publics. It is a collaborative approach to building understanding, and, although not perfectly balanced, it is a *moving equilibrium* in which both sides in the communication process have an opportunity to have input and change an issue. To revise this example, after research identifying tax cuts as an issue, a symmetrical politician would actually incorporate tax cuts into her belief system and offer ideas supporting those beliefs on the campaign trail.

In modern public relations, we often see a mixing of the public relations models among multiple tactics or communication tools within one public relations campaign. It is best to think of the models as theoretical constructs that, in implementation, become combined through the mixed motives of public relations. In most cases, public relations professionals not only want to aid their employer or client but also to assist the publics outside the organization to access and understand the inner workings of the firm. This **mixed-motive approach** is based on the real-world contingencies that impact public relations decisions, and the desire to facilitate communication on both sides of an issue, both for organizations and for publics.

Summary of the Models of Public Relations

In summary, the historical development of the field showed four distinct models of public relations, as identified by Grunig and Hunt. With this brief background in the history of public relations, you likely know enough about the models now to begin employing each in your public relations management. All are still in use in public relations practice today, and these terms are used in the academic literature and in public relations management. The one-way models are not based on social scientific research but on a simple dissemination of information. The two-way models are based on research, which is what makes them the two-way management model. In order of their development, the models are as follows:

- **Press agentry**. One-way (information) dissemination focusing on publicity for persuasion/attention.
- **Public information**. One-way (information) dissemination providing information.
- **Two-way asymmetrical**. Two-way (research), which is imbalanced in favor of persuading publics to support the organizations' interests.
- **Two-way symmetrical**. Two-way (research), which is more balanced in terms of creating mutual understanding; moving equilibrium.

Due to the *mixed-motives* inherent in the public relations process, public relations professionals will most likely use a combination of these models in public relations management. These models suggest an overall philosophy of public relations, while situations require different approaches. Therefore, it is also useful to have public relations strategies that reflect a contingency of varying approaches, as discussed later in this volume.

The Subfunctions of Public Relations

Before we delve deeper into the profession, we would like to introduce you to the subfunctions or specialties within public relations. Think of the public relations function as a large umbrella profession encompassing many subfunctions. Those subfunctions are often independent units within an organization, sometimes reporting to public relations and sometimes reporting to other organizational units such as legal, marketing, or human resources. Learning the subfunctions and the lexicon of terminology associated with this function is crucial to understanding how to manage an integrated and effective public relations function. The following subfunctions will be discussed in more detail later in this volume.

Although there are many subfunctions that make up public relations, most people would identify two major types, corporate and agency. **Corporate**, or "in-house," is a part of the organization or business. It functions to create relationships between an organization and its various publics. The second type of subfunction is associated with the **public relations agency**; its purpose is to assist organizations in a specific area of expertise.

Typical Corporate Public Relations Subfunctions

It is important to note that each subfunction may differ according to organizational structure and size, as we discuss in Chapter 5, "Organizational Factors Contributing to Excellent Public Relations." Sometimes the public relations subfunctions overlap and one department (or even one person) is responsible for many or all of these activities. Large organizations, particularly those with multiple locations doing business internationally, will sometimes have multiple units covering just one of these subspecialties in public relations. Oftentimes the public relations function is structured with a separate department handling each of the responsibilities.

Issues Management

Issues management is arguably the most important subfunction of public relations. Issues management is the forward-thinking, problem-solving, management-level function responsible for identifying problems, trends, industry changes, and other potential issues that could impact the organization. Issues management requires a formidable knowledge of research, environmental monitoring, the organization's industry and business model, and management strategy.

Media Relations

The media relations subfunction is likely the most visible portion of public relations that an organization conducts because it deals directly with external media. The media relations subfunction is a largely technical function, meaning it is based on the technical skill of producing public relations materials, or outputs. **Outputs** are often related to tactics, and examples of tactics include news releases, podcasts, brochures, video news releases for the broadcast media, direct mail pieces, photographs, Web sites, press kits, and social media (digital media).

Community Relations

As the name implies, the community relations subfunction is responsible for establishing and maintaining relationships with an organization's communities. Normally this territory implies a physical community, as in the borders of manufacturing facilities with their residential neighbors.

Philanthropy and Corporate Social Responsibility (CSR)

Oftentimes the functions of strategically donating funds or services and a corporate social responsibility endeavor are part of the public relations department's efforts. The Sarbanes-Oxley Act of 2002 requires corporations to hold to a code of ethics and to report on their socially responsible conduct. The public relations subfunction responsible for this reporting usually is called the CSR unit or department and often is combined with or managed by community relations.

Financial and Investor Relations

Many managers do not realize that public relations is the function responsible for writing an organization's annual report, quarterly earnings statements, and communicating with investors and market analysts. This type of public relations normally requires experience with accounting and financial reporting.

Marketing Communications

Marketing communications is also known as integrated marketing communications or integrated communications. Publicity and product promotion targeting the specific public consumers is the focus of this subfunction. Public relations strategies and tactics are used primarily through a press agentry model meant to increase awareness and persuade consumers to try or buy a certain product.

Government Relations and Public Affairs, Including Lobbying

The public affairs of an organization are the issues of interest to a citizenry or community about which an organization must communicate. Government relations handles maintaining relationships with both regulatory agencies and appointed and elected officials.

Internal Relations

Maintaining an effective and satisfied workforce is the job of internal relations. Public relations professionals who specialize in internal relations have the primary responsibilities of communicating with *intra*organizational publics, executives, management, administrative staff, and labor.

Typical Public Relations Agency Subfunctions

In addition to the general media relations activities offered by many public relations agencies, seven specializations or subfunctions commonly exist.

Crisis Management

Crisis management involves both planning for and reacting to emergency situations. Organizations have a need for quick response plans and fast and accurate information provided to the news media that public relations agencies specializing in crisis or risk management often provide and implement in the case of a crisis.

Lobbying

As an adjunct to the government relations or public affairs unit of the corporation, an external lobbying firm may also be hired. Lobbyists normally have expertise with the industry for which they are hired to communicate, and maintain relationships with legislators, press secretaries, and other governmental officials. They often provide educational documents, policy analysis, and research to those in government on behalf of clients.

Member Relations

The public relations subfunction known as member relations, as the name implies, is responsible for maintaining good relationships with members of an organization. These members may be alumni, donors, members of activist or support groups, or virtually any group distinguished by a commonality and requiring membership.

Development and Fund-Raising

The public relations subfunction of development fund-raising often overlaps with member relations in that it seeks to build support, particularly in the form of financial donations or government grants.

Polling and Research

Polling and research are carried out to such an extent within public relations that specialized firms exist to conduct these activities full time, usually on a contract or retainer basis. It should be noted, however, that very large organizations often have their own research "departments" within one or more public relations subfunctions.

Sports, Entertainment, and Travel Public Relations

Specialized forms of public relations exist as public relations subfunctions for each of these very large industries.

Advertising

Although advertising is a separate profession from public relations, it is usually employed as part of a public relations campaign.

Chapter Summary

This chapter has provided the basic knowledge of public relations models and subfunctions (both corporate and agency) necessary to understand and expand your knowledge of this vast and ever-changing profession. The models and subfunctions are those that generally comprise public relations, although they do vary by industry. The organization size, type, amount of government regulation, and even the organization's competition will determine whether it has all or some of these subfunctions present in-house, outsources them as needed, or relies on public relations agencies. Normally an organization will have a majority of the subfunctions on this list. They may be structured as part of the public relations department, or as independent units reporting to it, to another function, or to senior management.

Knowing the terminology related to the subfunctions helps to identify different forms of public relations and combinations of these efforts in practice. In order to achieve the most with public relations initiatives, it is important to know which subfunctions must exist, which work well with one another, and which need independence or autonomy. Further in the book, we will apply this knowledge to examine the structuring of the public relations department and subfunctions. We will examine how organizational structure has an impact on the models of public relations employed and the subfunctions that exist in practice.

CHAPTER 4

Public Relations as a Management Function

In the opening chapters, we provided an overview of public relations, including definitions, a brief history of the profession, and a description of the models and subfunctions common in the profession. In these chapters, public relations was defined as a unique management function that uses communication to help manage relationships with key publics. In this chapter, we will expound on this management function, explaining why companies need public relations and how the public relations function is comprised of specialized roles.

Functions of Management

Organizations usually have several management functions to help them operate at their maximum capacity: research and development, finance, legal, human resources, marketing, and operations. Each of these functions is focused on its own contribution to the success of the organization. Public relations' unique function is to help the organization develop and maintain relationships with all of its key publics and stakeholders by effectively communicating with these groups. Communication is key in maintaining a satisfactory, long-term, trusting relationships with publics and stakeholders.

As described earlier, public relations provides the greatest value to an organization when it is used *strategically*. But what does this really mean? Think of it this way: In an effective organization, all the major functions are linked together by a common set of strategies that tie in to an overall vision of the future and an underlying set of values. Perhaps a computer company has as its vision, "To become the low cost provider of computing power to the developing world." From this vision, senior management develops a set of strategies that address areas like sourcing, the manufacturing footprint, marketing, design, human resource development, and product distribution. When all the elements are in sync, the company grows in a steady, profitable manner.

An important component of this set of strategies is a *communication* strategy. For example, it will be critical that all employees in the organization understand that strategy and their role in executing it. Many business failures are ultimately attributable to the confusion caused by poor communication. How many times have you received poor customer service from an employee in a restaurant or retail outlet? In all likelihood, the organization that employed this worker intended for him or her to deliver good service to you. But somewhere along the line the communication flow broke down. Perhaps the employee's direct supervisor or the store manager was not an effective communicator. Whatever the cause, the end result is a dissatisfied customer and diminished loyalty to the relationship.

In addition to reaching employees, a successful organization must also communicate effectively with its customers, its suppliers, and if it is a public company, its shareholders. For each key public, a set of messages must be developed as well as a plan to reach the public in the most efficient way. If the company is targeting young people with its message, a high-impact article in the *Wall Street Journal* is going to completely miss the mark for this strategic public. If instead the public is high net-worth investors, a clever YouTube video may also not be the right answer.

Although public relations has a unique and important function within organizations, it is often practiced differently depending on the role the top communicator plays within the organization, as we discuss next.

Public Relations Roles

In general, public relations professionals can be communication managers who organize and integrate communication activities, or they can be communication technicians who primarily write and construct messages. Research in this area led to the identification of four specific roles: the technician role and three types of communication managers.

Most practitioners begin their careers as **communication technicians**. This role requires executing strategies with the communication tactics of news releases, employee newsletters, position papers, media placements, Web site content, speeches, blogs, and social media messaging. Practitioners in this role are usually not involved in defining problems and developing solutions, but base their tactics on the technical skill of writing. The **expert prescriber** is similar to the role a doctor performs with a patient: He or she is an authority on a particular industry, problem, or type of public relations and is given the primary responsibility to handle this function as a consultant or with little input or participation by other senior management. The **communication facilitator** is a boundary spanner who listens to and brokers information between the organization and its key publics. According to Cutlip, Center, and Broom, the goal of this role is "to provide both management and publics the information they need for making decisions of mutual interest."[1] The **problem-solving facilitator** collaborates with other managers to define and solve problems. This role requires that the professional is a part of the dominant coalition of the organization and has access to other senior managers. The problem-solving facilitator helps other managers think through organizational problems using a public relations perspective.

Research on these four roles found that the communication technician role was distinct from the other three roles and that the latter three roles were highly correlated.[2] In other words, an expert prescriber was also likely to fulfill the role of the communication facilitator and the problem-solving facilitator. To resolve the lack of mutual exclusiveness in the latter three roles, they were combined into one role: **communication manager**. The dichotomy between the communication technician and the communication manager more accurately explained the responsibilities of public relations practitioners within organizations.

Research indicates that practitioners in a predominantly technician role spend the majority of their time writing, producing, and placing communication messages.[3] Typically, those in this role are creative and talented with language and images. Their capacity to create and produce messages with powerful imagery and evocative language is very important to the execution of public relations tactics. However, technicians rarely have a seat at the management table and do not have a voice in the strategy of the organization. Once the strategy is decided, the technician is brought in to execute the deliverables (or tactics) in the strategy.

The communication manager is involved in the strategic thinking of an organization and must be able to conduct research and measurement and share data that informs better decisions for managing relationships with key publics. The communications manager thinks strategically, which means he or she will be focused on the efforts of the organization that contribute to the mutually beneficial relationships that help an organization achieve its bottom-line goals. These efforts are not limited to communication strategies, but include monitoring an organization's external environment, scanning for issues that might impact the organization, and helping an organization adapt to the needs of its stakeholders.

A study on excellence in the practice of public relations found that one of the major predictors of excellence was whether the role of the top public relations executive was a manager role or a technician role.[4] Those in the management role were much more likely to have a positive impact on the organization's public relations practice. In order for corporate communication to function strategically, the executive in charge of the function must have a place at the decision-making table.

The C-Suite

Virtually all organizations are run by a senior leadership team that is responsible for setting strategy and carrying out the organization's vision. Although publicly traded companies, as well as nonprofit organizations, may be governed ultimately by a board of directors, this board looks to the chief executive and his or her senior team to operate the company on a day-to-day basis.

The key functions in an organization include finance, headed by a chief financial officer (CFO); legal, which reports to the General Counsel; human resources, led by a chief personnel officer (CPO); information services, reporting to the chief information officer (CIO); marketing, often led by a chief marketing officer (CMO); and communication, which reports to the chief communications officer (CCO). These functional areas serve the operations of the company, which in some cases report to a president or chief operating officer. In many cases the CEO also is president/COO (chief operating officer) of the organization.

Although organizational structures vary from company to company, these basic functional areas are usually present in the senior team. In some cases, the communication function is subordinated under another area, such as marketing, legal, or human resources. When this is the case, it becomes more difficult for the senior communications leader to play a meaningful role in the strategic decision-making process. The communication function brings to the senior team a different perspective from these other areas. The legal function is focused primarily on compliance with the law; marketing is focused primarily on the company's competitive position with the customer; human resources (HR) is focused almost exclusively on employee compensation and development issues. In other words, communication is the only function with eyes on *all* the publics inside and outside of the organization, and should be included in strategic decision making.

Role of Communication in Decision Making

One of the common denominators for officers in the C-suite is the imperative to make good decisions that affect their ability to positively contribute to the goals of the organization. The ability to make good decisions often defines a valuable manager. To make good decisions, managers need good information. By definition, good information helps reduce uncertainty in making a decision. Rarely is a decision made with utter certainty, but managers need enough information to have confidence that their decisions will result in positive consequences. This information is provided as data regarding these various functions: product testing, market research, legal precedents, and financial statements. Since public relations' role is to help the organization develop and maintain good relationships, it must provide data or information about how the organization can achieve this. This is how strategic public relations earns its seat at the executive table.

The communication function looks at all the stakeholders in the organization and uses a variety of tools and tactics to enhance relationships with these publics. At its best, the communication function uses research and monitoring methods to keep a finger on the pulse of internal and external perceptions of the organization. It uses a variety of communication channels to enhance the organization's reputation. And most importantly it provides strategic counsel to the organization's leaders to help the team make better decisions.

Some have suggested that the communication function serves or should serve as the *corporate conscience*. They contend that communication leaders have a uniquely objective perspective that allows them to weigh the sometimes conflicting needs of different publics and to help the organization make more balanced decisions. Although there is much truth to this perspective, we add that the conscience of the organization, its moral obligation to do the right thing, is one that is shared by all who lead it, including the CEO, the board, and the senior management team.

As the top communication professional, the CCO has an important responsibility to ensure that all key stakeholders are given due consideration when critical decisions are made. In that regard, the CCO acts as the voice for many who are not in the room when choices are made. He or she must keep in mind the minority shareholders, overlooked employee segments, nongovernmental organizations, special interest groups, elected officials, community leaders, and others who may be affected by the decision and who have influential roles in their respective areas.

By providing this overarching perspective, the CCO does much more than deliver tactical communication products. This strategic counsel is what CEOs and other leaders are increasingly seeking in all members of the senior team. By delivering it, the CCO enhances the value of the function and ensures ongoing participation in charting the future course for the company.

Strategy and Profit Motivation

Public relations as a profession is often thought of as nothing more than a simple set of tactics. Far too often those in the profession are portrayed in the media and in popular culture as a group of empty-headed party planners or deceptive flacks willing to say anything to get publicity for their clients. The tools of the trade—news releases, press conferences, media events, employee newsletters—are considered as discrete tactics that rarely if ever are driven by an underlying strategy.

This, like other stereotypes, is simply not supported by fact. As practiced by most large organizations and agencies, public relations is an integral part of overall strategy. Communication programs are developed based on extensive research to address specific business objectives with stated outcomes, target audiences, and key messages. The results of these efforts can be measured, both qualitatively and quantitatively.

Think of it this way: When an organization develops a strategic plan, it usually does so with a relatively small number of key executives. These leaders look at the company's strengths, organization, challenging issues, and potential problems that could arise. They consider the organization's financial position, its growth prospects, its competitive position, and the changing landscape in which it operates.

When they have considered all of these factors, they map out a strategy that will build on the company's current strengths, address its relative areas of weakness, take advantage of opportunities, and prepare for looming threats. They may decide, for example, to be the low-cost provider in their industry segment. Or they may decide to take advantage of their expertise in new product development, or to exploit their superior distribution network.

At some point, the strategy must be executed by a much larger, geographically dispersed network of employees. This is where the communication strategy becomes crucial. If a company has a long track record of fighting with its employees over issues like pay, benefits, union representation, child care programs, or workplace safety, it will be much more difficult to call upon them to launch a new initiative aimed at improving customer service.

In large measure, an important role of the communication function team is to help balance the needs of all publics—employees, investors, customers, communities—as the organization makes key decisions. For example, assume that a company is facing financial difficulties due to declining market share in one part of the United States. They are faced with the decision of closing a regional plant since that level of manufacturing capacity is no longer needed. In the past, they simply might have turned to the public relations executive and said, "We're closing the Milwaukee plant. Try to put a good face on it." An organization that views the communication function as a strategic partner instead would say,

> We've got too much manufacturing capacity; operations is recommending that we close Milwaukee. We'd like you to take a look at the impact this will have with our employees, customers, and the community there and help us measure this as we examine the alternatives. There may be another choice that won't be as painful to the organization.

Balancing the needs of publics is just one facet of the impact public relations can have on achieving organizational goals. It obviously depends on the organization, but in almost every case, effective communication programs help drive strategy from conception to delivery. Successful internal communication programs can improve the ability of supervisors to motivate employees and build pride in the organization. Creative external communication programs can improve customer relationships, build brand recognition, encourage investor interest in a publicly traded company, and increase the effectiveness of traditional advertising and marketing efforts. Community outreach programs can help local residents appreciate the impact of a company on the surrounding area in which it operates. The impact of well-conceived strategic communication programs can be profound, and many companies have already benefitted by recognizing this importance and building upon the strengths public relations brings to the table.

In 2007, the Arthur W. Page Society, a membership organization of chief communications officers at the largest corporations, agency CEOs, and leading academics, produced a white paper called *The Authentic Enterprise*.[5] The report examined the evolving role of the senior communications executive in 21st-century business. According to this report, the role of the CCO is much broader than it was even a few years ago. The CCO of today and tomorrow must assert leadership in the following:

- Defining and instilling company values
- Building and managing multistakeholder relationships
- Enabling the enterprise with "new media" skills and tools
- Building and managing trust[6]

The communication executive does not own these responsibilities alone. They are shared with other members of the leadership team. But the communication executive can and should take a lead role in ensuring that these responsibilities are fulfilled by the organization.

Business Acumen

Having a seat at the decision-making table is not a right, it is a privilege. Think of it this way: If you were planning an extended trip to Mexico, you would probably want to brush up on your Spanish before embarking. You could probably get by without speaking Spanish, but you would be far more effective and much better accepted by the locals if you at least made an attempt to speak their native language.

It is not so different at the management table. There the participants are speaking the language of business. They are talking about margin performance and market capitalization and earnings growth. They are discussing business strategy and market share and competitive position. If you are not conversant in this terminology and the thinking behind it, you are at a distinct disadvantage as a team member.

The Page Society surveyed chief executive officers at large multinational corporations to determine how these CEOs viewed the role of the chief communications officer in a successful executive team. According to results reported in the *Authentic Enterprise* white paper, the most important attribute of an ideal CCO or communications manager was detailed knowledge of the business.

> This is far and away the most critical quality for a top communications executive. All CEOs believe that their businesses are large and complex entities, and that their companies cannot be communicated well if their top communications executives do not intimately understand them.[7]

Why does this understanding matter to CEOs and other members of the C-suite? In order to build persuasive communication programs that advance the objectives of the organization, the communication team, especially those who lead it, must first understand these objectives. They must also understand the context in which the organization is pursuing the objectives—both the business context and in external forces.

It is extremely important to build credibility with the publics you are trying to reach. When a spokesperson for an organization cannot convey anything beyond what is contained in carefully scripted talking points, the recipient of the information loses trust and confidence in the individual. Many reporters are reluctant to speak to a media relations professional if they believe that individual does not really understand the organization or the industry in which it operates. Communication professionals who have a thorough understanding of business, government, community issues, and the specific organization they serve are simply more valuable contributors to the overall effort.

Gaining knowledge about an organization and its business objectives does not mean gaining the expertise needed to be CFO, General Counsel, or head of accounting. There are some fundamental areas that are important to understand, general principles that will help communications professionals speak more credibly and work as more valued team members.

For example, publicly traded, for-profit companies all operate within a set of guidelines, standard benchmarks, and mileposts that help their publics gain insight about their financial health, prospects for growth, and competitive position. These measures can provide a quick snapshot of an organization's health in the same way that temperature, pulse rate, and blood pressure readings can give a physician a measure of a patient's well-being.

Maintaining Core Competencies

How does one gain much of the knowledge referenced earlier in addition to staying current with rapid changes? In some cases it makes sense to do so by pursuing additional educational opportunities. A number of courses are offered, for example, that teach basic finance for nonfinancial managers. Some communication professionals return to school to pursue a Master of Business Administration (MBA) or executive Master of Arts (MA).

Even without taking these steps, we can learn a great deal by simply following the business media, especially the *Wall Street Journal*; the major business magazines such as *Business Week*, *Fortune*, and *Forbes*; and broadcast media such as *CNBC* or *Fox Business*. The Internet also provides an endless source of information about individual companies and issues that affect all types of organizations and industries.

In the end, conversations with colleagues can provide incredible educational opportunities. The ability to listen, to ask insightful questions and to learn from others enables the communication professional to gain ample knowledge of the workings of business in general and a single company or organization more specifically. This knowledge, combined with an understanding of the industry and the ability to utilize communication expertise, provides a valuable combination of specialized abilities that can be used to benefit the entire organization.

Chapter Summary

Research on best practices of public relations sponsored by the International Association of Business Communicators suggests that excellent public relations occurs when the senior communications officer is part of the dominant coalition and has a presence in the C-suite.[8] When the public relations function is relegated to a communication technician role, it is not fulfilling its unique management function.

As mentioned previously, this status must be earned. Public relations professionals gain that access by providing essential information and counsel necessary for making important decisions. When these communication professionals have the advanced knowledge of strategic public relations, including research and evaluation, and demonstrate business acumen, they should be a part of that management team.

The next chapter will identify other organizational factors that also influence how public relations is practiced.

PART II

Organizations and Processes

CHAPTER 5

Organizational Factors Contributing to Excellent Public Relations

The International Association of Business Communicators (IABC) study on *Excellence in Public Relations and Communication Management* (*Excellence Study*) found three primary variables for predicting excellence: communicator knowledge, shared expectations about communication, and the character of organizations.[1] As mentioned in Chapter 4, public relations professionals who demonstrate greater management skills are more likely to participate in the C-suite. However, there are also organizational factors that influence the role that public relations plays in an organization. First, management must value the contributions that public relations can make to an organization; second, there must be a participative culture; and third, the organization must support diversity of people and ideas.

The *Excellence Study* found that communicator expertise was not enough to predict the best practices of public relations.[2] There had to be shared expectations between the communications function and senior management or dominant coalition. If the chief executive officer (CEO) and other top managers expect the public relations function to be strategic and contribute to the organization's bottom-line goals, they often require and support practices that included research and strategic planning and management rather than simply press releases and media placement. Such demand for advanced, two-way communication influences the actual practice in these organizations. It requires hiring and retaining professionals who can conduct research and analyze data that allows for more strategic practices.

Value of Public Relations

In order to gain a strategic management role in the organization, the public relations function must show its value to management. Hambrick said that coping with uncertainty is the basis for demonstrating value.[3] Technology, workflow, and external environments all contribute to creating uncertainties and, therefore, strategic contingencies. Excellent public relations should help an organization cope with the uncertainties. This can be achieved only with data and useful information. Information theory posits that data are only useful inasmuch as they reduce uncertainty.

When the public relations function provides information and feedback about stakeholder needs and expectations, it performs a critical task for the organization that is unique to its function. Saunders suggested that reducing uncertainty, performing a critical task, and being nonsubstitutable and pervasive all contribute to the influence of any function in an organization.[4] Influence is increased when public relations can show that it is unique and cannot be substituted by another function within the organization (it is *nonsubstitutable*) and when it is connected throughout the organization in such a way that it can help manage relationships with all the key stakeholders (it is *pervasive*). This unique task is much more critical to the organization when it is focused on establishing, maintaining, and repairing relationships with key stakeholders who are needed to help the organization be successful. When the function is simply publicity and media relations, these outcomes may be considered less critical and somewhat disposable when budgets become limited.

Organizational Culture

Organizations that scored high on the *Excellence Study* indicators had a culture *that was participative rather than authoritarian.* An organization's formal structure can often predict how much participation occurs in making decisions. Organizations that have very centralized and formal structures keep the decision-making function in the hands of a few top managers. Such hierarchical structures often have difficulty dealing with dynamic external environments, because their insulated structures are slower to respond and depend on few voices for making decisions. Robbins argued that centralization is the most detrimental factor impeding organizational effectiveness.[5] As L. Grunig summarized, decentralization "has the advantages of reducing the probability of information overload, providing more voices in the decision-making process, responding rapidly to new information, instilling motivation, and helping train managers to make good decisions."[6] Mintzberg identified two decentralization strategies to help organizations deal with dynamic environments: vertical and horizontal.[7] **Vertical decentralization** is delegating formal decision-making power downward through the chain of command, so that the person closest to the situation can make the appropriate decision. **Horizontal decentralization** occurs when decision-making power flows informally to people in operating core (people who directly produce the goods and services), technostructure (staff who design, maintain, and adjust work flow processes and structure), and support staff (people who provide indirect support to the rest of the organization: human resources, public relations, legal counsel).

To allow for participative cultures, organizations need to be relatively decentralized because organizational culture can actively shape an organization's management style and employees' day-to-day behaviors.[8] Culture has been defined in the organizational behavior literature as *the set of values, ideologies, and cognitions that are shared and understood through social interaction and that determine appropriate behavior.* Some organizations have strong (cohesive) cultures, whereas others can be relatively weak (ambiguous). Weak cultures have been tied to increases in political behavior because the values establishing expected behavior are not clearly understood.

For excellent public relations, the values that encourage participative decision making need to be present. The IABC study found the following variables described participative cultures: people feeling part of the team, working together, management caring about employees, everyone treated as equals, participation in decisions, management sharing power and responsibility, and the promotion of teamwork.[9] Organizations with authoritative cultures often correlated with centralized decision making and include such variables as rigid control by management, competition between departments, influence (who you know being more important than what you know), decisions based on authority, and fear of senior management. Not surprisingly, the *Excellence Study* found greater job satisfaction within *participative cultures.* More importantly, the organizations with participative cultures were also more likely to practice public relations that used two-way communication and research and that was more effective in helping the organization meets its goals and objectives.

Another important predictor of quality cultures in an organization is the treatment of women and employees from culturally diverse backgrounds. As the *Excellence Study* summarized, employees from diverse backgrounds provide a better picture of the reality outside the organization. Senior managers tend to be isolated from outside factors when they surround themselves with people just like them. Weick recommended *requisite variety* for senior management, which refers to the concept of striving to have inclusiveness in the management team that reflects outside publics.[10] Without variety among employees and leaders, an organization can get out of touch with the diversity of its stakeholders. This isolation can lead to awkward interactions and misunderstandings with these publics. Communication can be a difficult endeavor and requires shared experiences to eliminate misinterpretation. Diversity begins within the organization that demonstrates respect for all individuals. This respect for all individuals then extends to all stakeholders and becomes an essential condition for establishing mutually satisfactory relationships.

Organizational Structure

Organizational structure can, of course, have an impact on communication because of the reporting structures and flow of information in the organization. The typical structure of a simplified organization can be seen in Figure 5.1, with direct reporting relationships represented as solid lines.

In this figure, a service or information arm would likely be present, but our concern is to focus on the role of the chief communications officer (CCO) relative to the other members of the dominant coalition, or C-suite, all reporting to the CEO. Those executives may vary from organization to organization and industry to industry, depending on the size of the pursuit, how complex it is, and how many sites it operates. Imagine that there are many levels of employees as we move down the organization who are not represented in this chart.

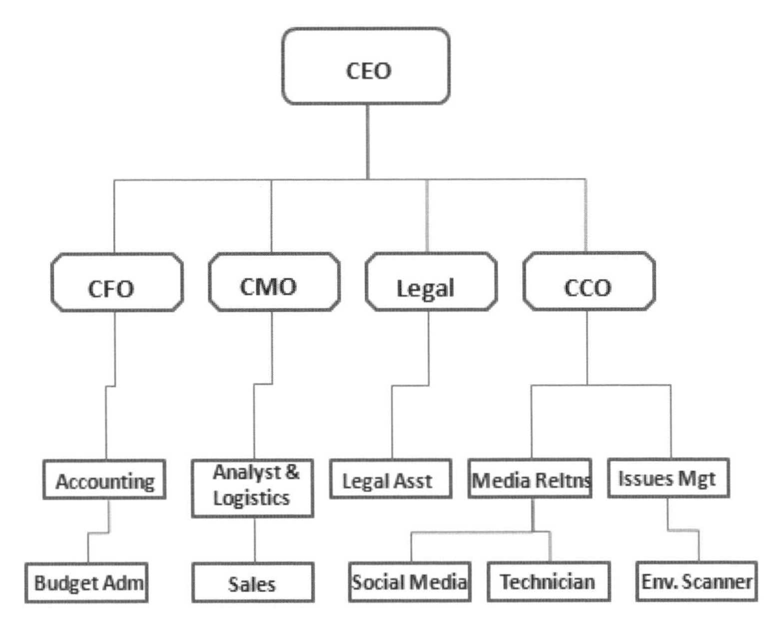

Figure 5.1. Simple organizational structure.

In an organization with a production component, such as any manufacturing-based organization, a more complex understanding of the organization begins to emerge. We can see in Figure 5.2 how the chief production officer, or CPO, is added into the dominant coalition mix, alongside the chief finance officer (CFO), chief marketing officer (CMO), legal counsel, and CCO.

Most organizations of this type would have a very wide base of hourly production workers reporting to the CPO, as well as numerous supervisors and administrative staff of various kinds and levels throughout the chart. Simplifying it to the direct-reporting relationships involved in the management chain of command allows us to see how the corporate communication function both reports to the CEO and interacts with the rest of the dominant coalition across functional areas.

Finally, the public relations agency structure can vary a great deal from firm to firm, but it is based upon a consulting relationship to the client. A direct reporting relationship with a senior account executive or vice president of accounts is normally established, as well as a dotted-line, or as-needed, less frequent and more informal reporting relationship

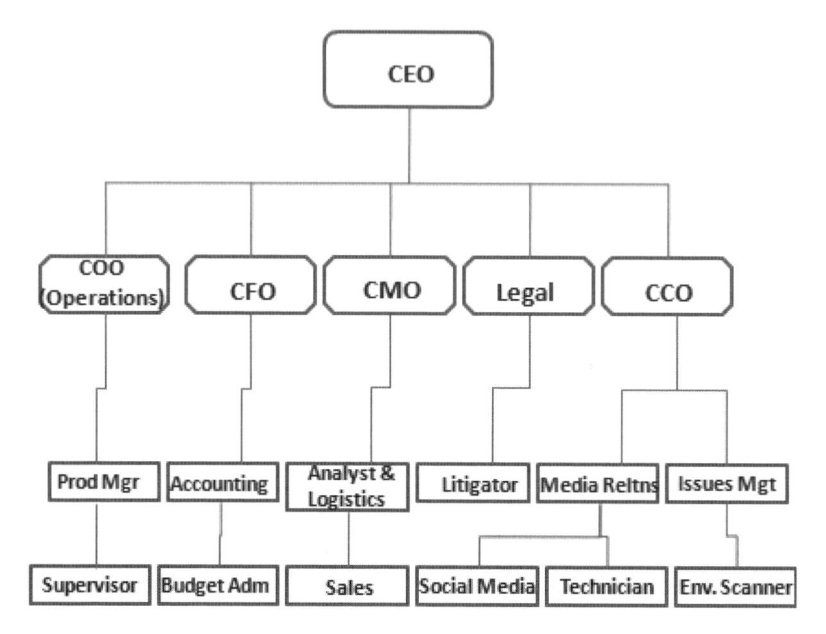

Figure 5.2. Organizational structure with a production (manufacturing) component.

between an account executive (AE) and the lead of the agency, often the president or CEO. (See Figure 5.3 for an example of public relations agency structure.)

The AE would have more routine contact with the client on a day-to-day working basis, and the CEO would have only infrequent but important contact with the client. The senior AE would normally oversee the account and all of its operations. The agency would provide creative services, such as graphic design and layout, media relations activities and story placement, and some marketing promotions activities for the client. Some firms have a relationship with advertising agencies, or have an in-house liaison for working with advertising initiatives. The technical skills role in public relations is normally an entry-level position focusing on writing and the creation of tactics or messages that will be disseminated. The larger portion of the chart on the bottom level would be comprised of many technicians of varying production specialties, and also normally employs administrative staff and some interns.

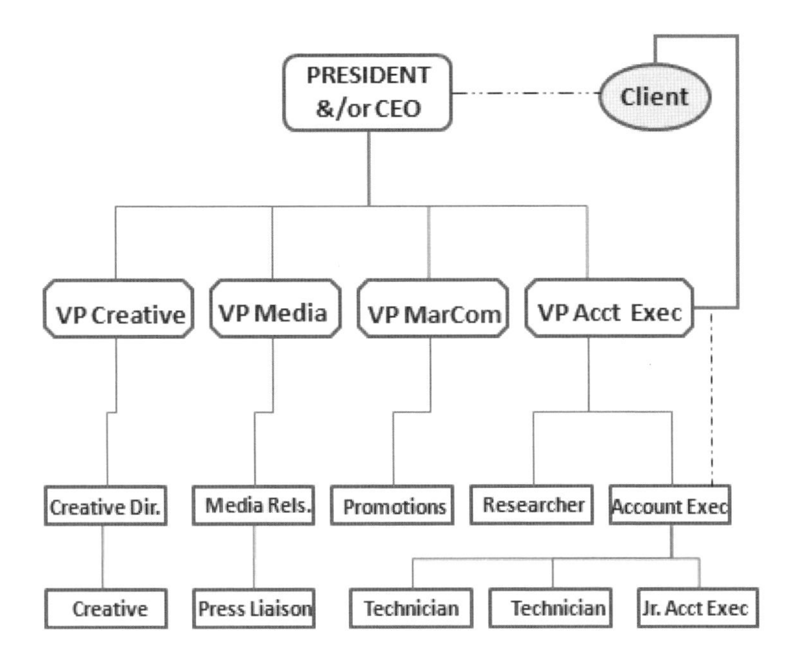

Figure 5.3. Public relations agency structure.

Chapter Summary

In this chapter, we reviewed findings from the *Excellence Study* and other sources about the important impact that organizational culture and structure have on the communication function, the view the CEO holds of the public relations practice, and the reasons for encouraging a participative organizational culture as a factor that builds effectiveness. Research supports the notion that public relations is more effective for organizations when it is valued by the dominant coalition or C-suite, the organizational structure is relatively decentralized allowing decision-making autonomy, and there is a direct reporting line between the CCO and the CEO. Further, the *Excellence Study* argued that the best organizations value participation and diversity.

Obviously, these organizational factors are going to vary from organization to organization, and the structure and organizational cultural elements often reflect the unique needs of each.[11] Some may be more centralized and more participative in culture, whereas others might be more decentralized but less participative.

CHAPTER 6

How Public Relations Contributes to Organizational Effectiveness

Contemporary public relations as noted in earlier chapters is defined as existing within the management of the organization. As public relations has shifted from an emphasis on the technical role of the communicator to the strategic communication role of the manger, the public relations professional has had to become educated in how organizations are managed. This chapter introduces you to several different management theories that help define organizational success and the public relations role in managing that success.

Management theory has defined organizational effectiveness in a number of ways. Early theories of management stressed meeting goals as measures of effectiveness. This approach proved to be rather simplistic and did not recognize the interconnectedness of organizations with their environments. A systems model approach was developed as a reaction to the limitations of the goal-attainment perspective. However, the systems approach tends to be too abstract to measure effectiveness. A third approach, which recognizes the dependency of the organization on its environment, places specific focus on key constituents and is more measurable because of its focus on relationships with these stakeholders. This approach, which is often called **stakeholder management**, recognizes the value of strategic constituents to the success of any organization, and recognizes that the interests of these stakeholders often conflict. Each impacts on how public relations is practiced within the organization.

Goal Attainment Approach

Traditionally, an organization's effectiveness has been defined in terms of attaining goals.[1] In the earliest theories of organizational behavior, organizations were viewed as rational institutions whose primary purpose is to accomplish objectives. The more efficiently and effectively an organization can achieve its goals, the more successful it is according to this approach. Quite often, the bottom-line goals of organizations are focused on profitability.

Financial Goals

One way to look at the success of organizations is to assess their size relative to competitors. This type of measurement is usually done by looking first at annual revenues, the sum total of all products or services sold to customers. But this may not be the most meaningful measure since some very large companies are not always successful. Financial analysts usually look at other ratios to determine financial health. They look at profitability in a number of ways to assess the return that the company is generating for its owners—the shareholders—for each dollar of investment in the business, a concept known as *ROI* or **return on investment**. In doing so, they consider the **gross margins** the company achieves, which are the revenues generated from the sale of its products minus the cost of those goods. They also consider the organization's **net earnings**, which are the profits remaining after all interest, taxes, and other costs such as depreciation are factored in.

These net earnings are then divided by all the shares of stock outstanding to determine **earnings per share**, or EPS. This EPS number provides a good ratio for making comparisons to other companies regardless of their size. Financial analysts eagerly await the earnings numbers when publicly traded companies release these results each quarter, as they are required to do by the U.S. Securities and Exchange Commission (SEC). Analysts estimate what they expect a company to earn, sometimes a year or more in advance of the actual results. When companies exceed these estimates, their stock prices generally increase—sometimes dramatically—after the release of earnings. When they disappoint the analysts and underachieve on projected earnings, their share prices can plummet.

Another measure of size is **market capitalization**. That measure is determined by multiplying the current price of a single share of a company's stock by all the shares outstanding. In some cases, this "market cap" number may be significantly higher than the annual revenues a company achieves. In such cases the financial markets believe that the company has growth potential far in excess of its current sales. Companies with market caps far higher than revenues are more highly valued than companies whose market caps are similar to or much lower than annual revenues. Companies work to achieve higher valuation by delivering consistent performance, meeting or exceeding earnings estimates, and providing a credible growth story that is supported by the facts.

There are countless other financial measures. However, the most important thing to remember is that communicators have a special responsibility to educate themselves on the measures that are deemed most important by their colleagues in other functions. That includes more than the numbers. They must also understand the business challenges that are most pressing to the company.

For nonprofit public relations, the most important measures may relate to the donor community or to the volunteer network on which the organization relies. For governmental public relations it may require an increase in knowledge of policies, legislative initiatives, sources of tax revenues, or judicial rulings that will have an impact on the department's operations.

Limitations of Goal Attainment Approach

One critical limitation to the goal attainment approach to evaluate organizational effectiveness is that it does not take into consideration the very human nature of organizations, nor the outside influences that affect the efforts to reach these goals. People are not cogs in a wheel, and a manager could become easily frustrated with the unrealistic expectation that organizations can run as smoothly as a piece of machinery. This makes engagement of employees a problem for the public relations professional, and his or her focus is often more on goal attainment than maintaining positive relations with publics.

Robbins criticized the goal-attainment approach because it does not consider the political or power-control nature of organizations and how they choose goals.[2] Most organizations are composed of coalitions, which lobby for goals that benefit them or their function in the organization. He argued that the interests of decision makers and of their organization are not always congruous and that the typical manager tries to increase the size and scope of his or her domain regardless of the effect on the organization as a whole. He contended that organizational interests are subordinated to the special self-interests of different groups within the organization. The most powerful of these coalitions are successful in defining the organization's goals, and meeting these goals adds power and influence to these coalitions. In addition, there is evidence that the goals of each coalition may not directly reflect the needs and purposes of the organization.

Another criticism leveled at the goal-attainment approach is that it viewed organizations as rational and mechanical systems that could control whether these goals were reached. As scholars noted, these management theories presumed that the organizations were closed systems that had autonomy from and control of their environments.[3] However, organizations are interconnected with their external environments.

Systems Theory Approach

The view of organizations as open social systems that must interact with their environments in order to survive is known as the **systems theory approach**. Organizations depend on their environments for several essential resources: customers who purchase the product or service, suppliers who provide materials, employees who provide labor or management, shareholders who invest, and governments that regulate. According to Cutlip, Center, and Broom, public relations' essential role is to help organizations adjust and adapt to changes in an organization's environment.[4]

The open-systems approach was first applied by Katz and Kahn, who adapted General Systems Theory to organizational behavior.[5] This approach identifies organizational behavior by mapping the repeated cycles of input, throughput, output, and feedback between an organization and its external environment. Systems receive input from the environment either as information or in the form of resources. The systems then process the input internally, which is called throughput, and release outputs into the environment in an attempt to restore equilibrium to the environment. The system then seeks feedback to determine if the output was effective in restoring equilibrium. As can be seen, the systems approach focuses on the means used to maintain organizational survival and emphasize long-term goals rather than the short-term goals of the goal-attainment approach.

Theoretically, systems can be considered either open or closed. Open organizations exchange information, energy, or resources with their environments, whereas closed systems do not. In reality, because no social systems can be completely closed or open, they are usually identified as relatively closed or relatively open. The distinction between closed and open systems is determined by the level of sensitivity to the external environment. Closed systems are insensitive to environmental deviations, whereas open systems are responsive to changes in the environment.

The systems approach is an external standard that measures effectiveness based on long-term growth or sustainability. Effective systems are characterized by a steady state that systems theorists call **homeostasis** in order to "avoid the static connotations of equilibrium and to bring out the dynamic, processual, potential-maintaining properties of basically unstable . . . systems."[6] If an organization is able to maintain homeostasis, which includes not just survival but also growth, then it is *effective*. This perspective is broader and more comprehensive than the goal-attainment approach because it is not limited to measuring effectiveness as meeting goals determined by powerful internal coalitions that may or may not be propitious for the whole organization. Pfeffer and Salancik defined effectiveness as "how well an organization is meeting the demands of the various groups and organizations that are concerned with its activities."[7]

Most effective organizations, according to systems theory, adapt to their environments. Pfeffer and Salancik described the environment as the events occurring in the world that have any effect on the activities and outcomes of an organization. Environments range from "static" on one extreme to "dynamic" on the other. Static environments are relatively stable or predictable and do not have great variation, whereas dynamic environments are in a constant state of flux. Because environments cannot be completely static or constantly changing, organizations have varying levels of dynamic or static environments.

Organizations that exist in dynamic environments must be open systems in order to maintain homeostasis. Because dynamic environments are constantly changing, they create a lot of uncertainty about what an organization must do in order to survive and grow. The key to dealing with uncertainty is *information*. An open organization monitors its environment and collects information about environmental deviations that is labeled as **input**. Input can also be thought of as a form of feedback. The most important information is negative input, according to systems theorists, because this information alerts the organization to problems that need to be corrected. *Negative* input tells the organization that it is doing something wrong and that it must make adjustments to correct the problem; *positive* input tells the organization that it is doing something right and that it should continue or increase that activity.

Organizations then organize and process this information to formulate solutions or responses to these changes. As Cutlip, Center, and Broom noted, open systems use information to respond to environmental changes and adjust accordingly. The adjustments affect the structure or process of the organization, or both. The structure is what the organization *is*, whereas process is what the organization *does*. Adjustments are "intended to reduce, maintain, or increase the deviations."[8] For example, an organization can alter its structure by downsizing to remain competitive. Other organizations may change their processes in order to adhere to new environmental laws. Processing positive and negative input to adjust to environmental change is called **throughput**. In the throughput of information, the organization analyzes it and tailors it strategically to fit with the organization's goals, values, and within the relationship context it holds with publics.

After an organization adapts to environmental changes, its actions and messages represent its output. The automobile industry is constantly enticing car consumers to try the latest models, hoping that it has responded to changing expectations. Recently, many auto manufacturers have attempted to color their products as "green" or environmentally friendly. However, messages are not enough. If the cars are not really friendlier to the environment, then these messages eventually will fall on skeptical ears and impugn the credibility of the organization. An organization measures the effectiveness of its output by seeking feedback. If its actions and messages were not effective then the process is repeated until the appropriate solution is found. If the organization is not able to adapt to the environmental variation then it will eventually cease to exist. The public relations professional engaged in an organization that takes a systems approach is continually focusing on feedback as a way of measuring organizational success.

The public relations professional can use the academic concept of systems theory to implement protocols for regular feedback to the organization, thereby aligning it with the desires of publics in its environment. This theory can also be useful in understanding the role of research and feedback in creating a thoroughly analyzed and consistent strategy (the throughput stage of information in systems theory). The analysis of information and creation of strategy known as throughput helps to conceptualize and justify not only the research budget of the public relations department but also the need for making decisions that strategically align the public communications of an organization with the information needed by publics. The practical implementation of this approach keeps public relations from being used as a simple publicity function, and places the function squarely in the strategic planning process.

Systems theory, however, is not without some shortcomings. The first shortcoming relates to measurement, and the second is the issue of whether the means by which an organization survives really matter. Robbins noted that one criticism of this approach is that its focus is on "the means necessary to achieve effectiveness rather than on organizational effectiveness itself."[9] Measuring the means, or process, of an organization can be very difficult when compared to measuring specific end goals of the goal-attainment approach.

Stakeholder Management Approach

The stakeholder management approach adds focus to the systems approach by building "strategic constituencies." Robbins declared that an organization should be concerned only with the "strategic constituencies"[10] in the environment who can threaten the organization's survival. This approach recognizes that an organization must deal with external and internal publics who can constrain or enhance its behavior.

Although organizations would prefer to have complete autonomy, they are often confronted with constraints and controls. Constraints are often considered undesirable because they "cost money—to comply with regulations or to make changes to accommodate pressure groups,"[11] and they "restrict creativity and adaptation."[12] However, it is inevitable that an organization meets with some constraints, especially in heavily regulated industries. Examples include labor strikes, government regulations, boycotts, and protests by special interest groups.

To be effective, an organization "must be aware of environmental publics such as customers, suppliers, governmental agencies, and communities and interact successfully with them."[13] They must also be aware of the internal publics, such as employees and labor unions, who can affect or be affected by the organization. The relationship between an organization and its stakeholders is called **interdependence** in systems theory literature. Although these interdependent relationships limit autonomy, good relationships with stakeholders limit it less than bad relationships. When organizations collaborate with key stakeholders the end result is often an increase of autonomy. Good relationships are developed when an organization voluntarily interacts with its stakeholders to find mutually beneficial solutions. Poor relationships can result in forced compliance to restrictions and regulations. When organizations voluntarily establish relationships with stakeholders they have more autonomy because they are not forced into these relationships.

The Stakeholder Management Process

Stakeholder management centers on a six-step process as summarized in Figure 6.1. The process requires that the public relations function first identify key stakeholders, describe their stakes in the organization, and determine if those stakes are significant. Once these steps have been accomplished, opportunities and challenges must be evaluated, determine the organization's responsibility to the stakeholder, and finally create relationship strategies.

1. Identify stakeholders.
2. Describe the stakes.
3. Consider the significance of stakes/claims.
4. Evaluate opportunities.
5. Consider responsibilities to stakeholders.
6. Consider relationship-enhancing strategies and actions.

Figure 6.1. Six steps in the process of stakeholder management.

Step 1: Identify the Stakeholders

According to Carroll, the stakeholder management process begins by identifying the stakeholders.[14] Establishing these relationships is often advantageous for both organization and publics, as the relationships can be genuinely developed before they are urgently needed in a crisis situation. (In the next chapter we will show you how to construct a stakeholder map and analyze the connections between the organization and its publics.)

Step 2: Describe the Stakes

The next step is describing the stakes or claims these groups have in the organization. A **stake** is an interest or a share in the performance or success of an organization. Employees, shareholders, and other groups may have such a stake. A stakeholder group could also assert a **claim** on the organization if it believes the organization owes them something. For example, environmental groups believe that corporations have a responsibility to care for the environment. The legitimacy of the stakeholders' stake or claim must also be considered. The legitimacy of the stake or claim will be influenced by what the organization values. When management gives profits highest priority, then the interests of the owners, including shareholders, is paramount. Other values, such as concern for the environment, good working conditions, and customer satisfaction, would consider the needs of other stakeholders in an organization holding these values in addition to a profit motive. Stakes or claims can also be in conflict with each other. For example, the pressure to report profits may lead an organization to lay off employees, which would conflict with the benefits of having greater employee morale. The difficult part of stakeholder management is being able to manage the potential conflicts of interests among the stakeholders, and it is often a challenging pursuit to achieve a balance of stakeholder interests.

Step 3: Consider the Significance

The third step is to consider the significance of the stakeholders' stake or claim. Mitchell, Agle, and Wood developed a comprehensive model that included the stakeholder attributes of legitimacy, power, and urgency as a way to evaluate the priority of stakeholders.[15] **Legitimacy** is determined by whether the stakeholder has a legal, moral, or presumed claim that can influence the organization's behavior, direction, process, or outcome. Stakeholders have **power** when they can influence other parties to make decisions the party would not have otherwise made. **Urgency** exists when the issue is immediately pressing (time sensitive) or when it is critical to the stakeholder. They used the combination of the three attributes to develop a prioritization strategy. Accordingly, *latent* stakeholders possess only one of the attributes; *expectant* stakeholders possess two attributes, and *definitive* stakeholders possess all three attributes. The more attributes stakeholders possess, the more critical their claim.

Step 4: Evaluate Opportunities

The fourth step is evaluating the opportunities and challenges the stakeholders present to the organization. According to Carroll, opportunities and challenges might be viewed as the potential for cooperation and the potential for threat. Opportunities are situations that advance the goals of an organization if they are seized, whereas challenges usually have to be overcome. Stakeholders can either help or hinder the efforts of an organization, and each group should be analyzed according to what it brings to the table in each situation.

Step 5: Consider Responsibilities to Stakeholders

The fifth step is to consider the responsibilities an organization has to its stakeholders, meaning the ethical obligations that are held with regard to decision making, disclosure, and maintaining long-term relationships that engender trust. Beyond the assessment of opportunities and threats, what legal, moral, citizenship, community, and philanthropic responsibilities should be followed in order for the organization to be considered a valuable member of society?

These responsibilities include the financial, environmental, and social impact the organization has on society as a whole, and consist of such areas as fiscal accountability to shareholders, safe work environments for employees, and reduced negative impact on the environment. More is said on the ethics of decision making elsewhere in this book, and using a philosophical framework to rigorously analyze responsibilities is helpful in practicing effective public relations. Such a framework leads to more understandable, consistent, and defensible decisions than a more relativistic ethical approach that can be attacked as capricious, biased, or worse. Determining organizational values can help to articulate the various responsibilities that decisions should seek to fill.

Step 6: Consider Relationship Enhancement

The final step is to consider the strategies and actions an organization should take to enhance its relationships with key stakeholders. Since that is the primary function of public relations, the responsibility for developing strategic plans should fall on its shoulders. Public relations professionals have been trained in a strategic process that focuses the organization's communications and actions toward enhancing these relationships.

Employing stakeholder management techniques in professional practice means that the public relations professional holds the reins and responsibility for the relationships that are the very lifeblood of an organization. Using stakeholder management allows the professional to accurately assess the situation, prioritize resources, and make decisions that are the most strategic, helping to build long-term relationships with the most important publics and enhancing organizational effectiveness.

Chapter Summary

It is important to understand how organizations define their success because they place more value on the functions that contribute to that success and tend to reward those efforts the most. This chapter identified three ways that organizations evaluate their effectiveness. Most organizations set goals and measure themselves against those goals. These short-term benchmarks are easier to measure, but may blind the organization from the forest for the trees. An organization must also consider its long-term sustainability and growth, and a systems theory approach helps an organization keep its eye on the horizon. Key constituents are essential to reaching immediate goals and sustaining long-term growth. A stakeholder management approach helps an organization understand how critical these constituents are to meeting the purpose of the organization. Using the six steps of the stakeholder management process, public relations professionals can better understand challenges facing the organization and can help to integrate the interests of those stakeholders into management. Doing so strategically aligns the policy of the organization, allowing it to build more enduring relationships with publics and integrate public relations as a primary contributor to the bottom line and overall organizational effectiveness.

CHAPTER 7

Identifying and Prioritizing Stakeholders and Publics

One of the most important steps in strategic and effective public relations is accurately identifying the publics with which you want to build mutually beneficial relationships. A popular axiom for public relations is that there is no such thing as a "general public." In other words, an organization has a variety of key groups who bring different expectations for their relationship with the organization. These differences help an organization segment its publics into groups with similar values and expectations and to focus communication strategies.

Stakeholder Management and Prioritizing Publics*

Experts in stakeholder management and public relations have provided many different ways of identifying key stakeholders or publics. At the heart of these attempts is the question, "How much attention does each stakeholder group deserve or require?"

Because it is impossible that all stakeholders will have the same interests in and demands on the organization, Winn specified that stakeholder management be about managing stakeholders' potentially conflicting interests.[1] Once organizations have identified their stakeholders, there is a struggle for attention: who to give it to, who to give more to, and who to ignore. Sacrificing the needs of one stakeholder for the needs of the other is a dilemma with which many organizations struggle. When these conflicts arise it is important to the success of the organization that it has prioritized each stakeholder according to the situation.

---

* This section is revised with permission from Rawlins (2006).

This chapter will provide a model that moves from the broadest attempts at identifying all stakeholders, to the more specific need of identifying key publics for communication strategies. The model is situational, and priority of stakeholders and publics will change according to the situation.

Defining Stakeholders and Publics

A **stakeholder** is a group or individual who is affected by or can affect the success of an organization.[2] The definition has been expanded to include groups who have interests in the corporation, regardless of the corporation's interest in them. Employees, customers, shareholders, communities, and suppliers are those most commonly classified as stakeholders within an organization

Grunig and Repper differentiated the terms "stakeholder" and "public" in the following way: Organizations choose stakeholders by their marketing strategies, recruiting, and investment plans, but "publics arise on their own and choose the organization for attention."[3] This classification relied on John Dewey's definition of a public: That it is a group of people who face a similar problem, recognize the problem, and organize themselves to do something about it.[4] Therefore, publics organize from the ranks of stakeholders when they recognize an issue and act upon it.

Stakeholder Linkages to the Organization

Organization should attempt to identify *all* stakeholders before narrowing them by their attributes. One way to do this is by considering how these groups are linked to the organization. A model by Grunig and Hunt breaks these links into four groups by linkage: enabling, functional, diffused, and normative stakeholders (see Figure 7.1).[5]

- **Enabling stakeholders** have some control and authority over the organization, such as stockholders, board of directors, elected officials, governmental legislators and regulators, and so on. These stakeholders provide an organization with resources and necessary levels of autonomy to operate. When enabling

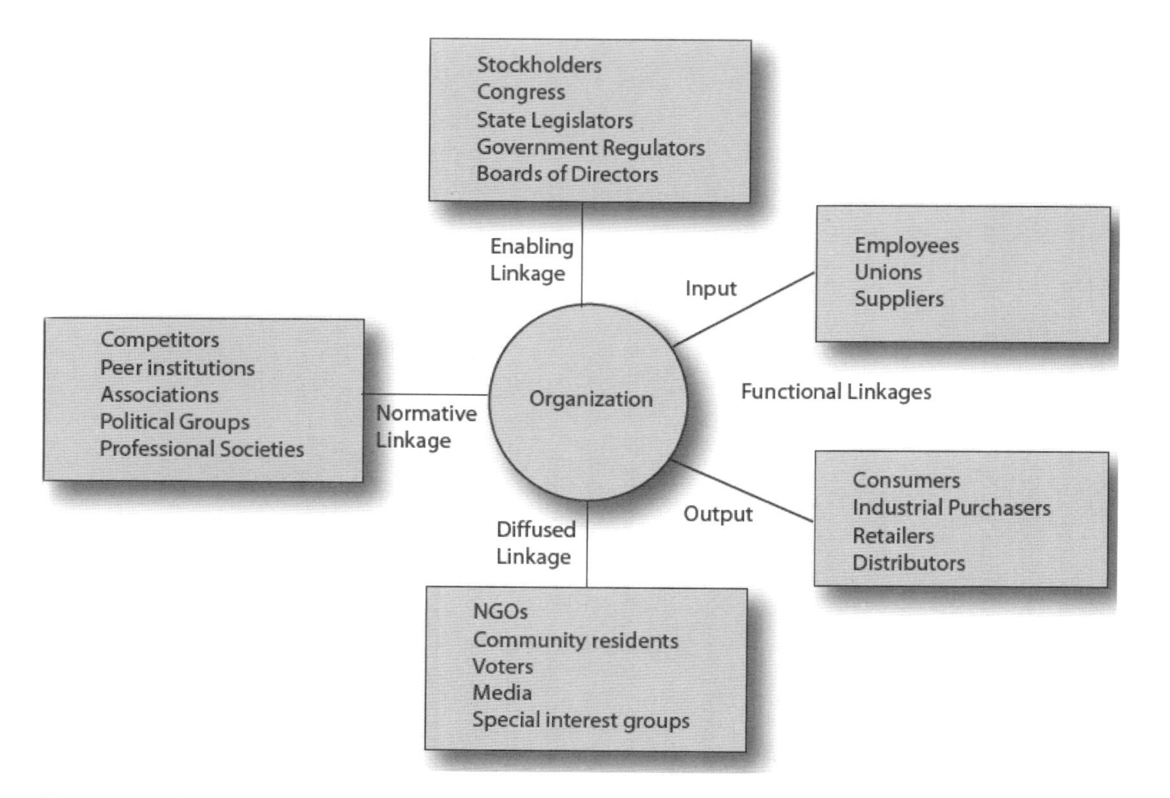

Figure 7.1. Grunig's organizational linkage model.

Source: Rawlins (2006) adapted and used with permission from Grunig.

relationships falter, the resources can be withdrawn and the autonomy of the organization limited, restricted, or regulated.

- **Functional stakeholders** are essential to the operations of the organization and are divided between *input*—providing labor and resources to create products or services (such as employees and suppliers)—and *output*—receiving the products or services (such as consumers and retailers).
- **Normative stakeholders** are associations or groups with which the organization has a common interest. These stakeholders share similar values, goals, or problems and often include competitors that belong to industrial or professional associations.
- **Diffused stakeholders** are the most difficult to identify because they include publics who have infrequent interaction with the organization, and become involved based on the actions of the organization. These are the publics that often arise in times of a crisis; linkages include the media, the community, activists, and other special interest groups.

Going through the linkage model should help an organization identify all its stakeholders. The diffused linkage stakeholders would be different according to situation, but the enabling, functional, and normative linkage stakeholders are likely to be constant.

The Situational Theory of Publics Predicts Active or Passive Behavior

Grunig developed a situational theory of publics to explain and predict why some publics are active and others are passive. Within the stakeholder categories he notes that situational theory can identify which publics will "communicate actively, passively, or not at all about organizational decisions that affect them."[6]

Those publics who do not face a problem are **nonpublics**, those who face the problem but do not recognize it as a problem are **latent publics**, those who recognize the problem are **aware publics**, and those who do something about the problem are **active publics**. He identified three variables that explain why certain people become active in certain

	High Involvement	Low Involvement
Problem-Facing Behavior High Problem Recognition Low Constraint Recognition	*Active Public*	*Active/Aware Public*
Constrained Behavior High Problem Recognition HighConstraint Recognition	*Aware/Active Public*	*Latent/Aware Public*
Routine Behavior LowProblem Recognition Low Constraint Recognition	*Active (Reinforcing) Public*	*None/Latent Public*
Fatalistic Behavior LowProblem Recognition High Constraint Recognition	*Latent Public*	*Non Public*

Figure 7.2. Grunig's situational theory of publics.

Source: Rawlins (2006) adapted and used with permission from Grunig.

situations: level of involvement, problem recognition, and constraint recognition (see Figure 7.2).

Level of involvement is measured by the extent to which people connect themselves personally with the situation. However, people do not seek or process information unless they recognize the connection between them and a problem, which is the level of **problem recognition**. Whether people move beyond information processing to the information seeking behavior of active publics often depends on whether they think they can do something about the problem. **Constraint recognition** is the level of personal efficacy a person believes that he or she holds, and the extent to which he or she is having an impact on the issue is possible. Those who think that nothing can be done have high constraint recognition and are less compelled to become active in the resolution of the problem. Another consideration, **referent criteria**, is the guideline that people apply to new situations based on previous experiences with the issue or the organization involved.

Active publics are likely to have high levels of involvement and problem recognition, and lower levels of constraint recognition. Because they recognize how the problem affects them and they think they can do something about it, Grunig theorized that this public will actively seek information and act on that information. Aware publics will process information and might act, but are limited by lower levels of involvement and problem recognition, or higher levels of constraint recognition. Latent publics are not cognizant of how an issue involves them or don't see it as a problem. They are simply not active on the issue. This public could become active or aware as information changes its cognitions about the issue.

Grunig tested the theory using problems that would create active and passive publics. He found four kinds of publics:

1. **All-issue publics**, which are active on all issues.
2. **Apathetic publics**, which are inattentive to all issues.
3. **Single-issue publics**, which are active on a small subset of the issue that only concerns them.
4. **Hot-issue publics**, which are active on a single issue that involves nearly everyone and which has received a lot of media attention.

To summarize this step, active publics will have more priority over aware and inactive publics because their urgency is greater. Whether stakeholders will become active publics can be predicted by whether the problem involves them, whether they recognize the problem, and whether they think they can do anything about it.

One dimension missing from this model is whether the public is supportive or not. Each of these groups could be supportive or threatening, and stakeholder strategies would be contingent on the level of support. A comprehensive model of stakeholder prioritization should also identify whether active or aware publics are supportive or threatening.

Communication Strategy With Stakeholders

Stakeholders who are also active publics become the obvious top priority publics. Although it would be convenient if active publics were always definitive stakeholders, human nature precludes this from happening in a constant and predictable way. Therefore, an organization must develop strategies to help mediate issues with priority publics. These strategies will depend on whether the stakeholders are supportive or nonsupportive and active or inactive. Therefore, you would develop strategies based on four groups, advocate stakeholders (active and supportive), dormant stakeholders (inactive and supportive), adversarial stakeholders (active and nonsupportive), and apathetic stakeholders (inactive and nonsupportive), as shown in Figure 7.3:

1. **Advocate stakeholders**. This is the group that you want involved in supportive actions such as third-party endorsements, letter-writing campaigns, donations, investments, and attendance at functions. Communication should be action and behavior oriented.
2. **Dormant stakeholders**. This is a group that is not ready to be involved. If inactivity is due to lack of knowledge, messages should focus on creating awareness and understanding of the issues that affect them. If the publics are aroused, but not active, then communication should address potential causes of apathy by reducing perceptions of constraints or using affective cues to increase emotional attachment.

3. **Adversarial stakeholders**. The initial response to this group is to be defensive. However, defensive communication will not work on this group, it will only entrench them in their position. Defensive communication is better intended for aroused publics who have not decided whether they are supportive or not. Instead, organizations should use conflict resolution strategies that involve nonsupportive stakeholders to seek win-win solutions.
4. **Apathetic stakeholders**. Again, the gut reaction to this group is to ignore it. But if this group faces an issue but is not aware of it or does not see its resonance yet, it may still move to an aroused, then aware, and then active public. A better strategy is to increase awareness of the issue with an invitation to collaborate with the organization on the issue before it becomes a problem or crisis. Since it would be difficult to get this group involved, most of the communication effort should be focused on increasing the salience of the issue and invitations for involvement.

Once strategies have been developed that address the stakeholders, there is one last prioritization step. According to Wilson, there are three types of publics involved in communication strategies: key publics,

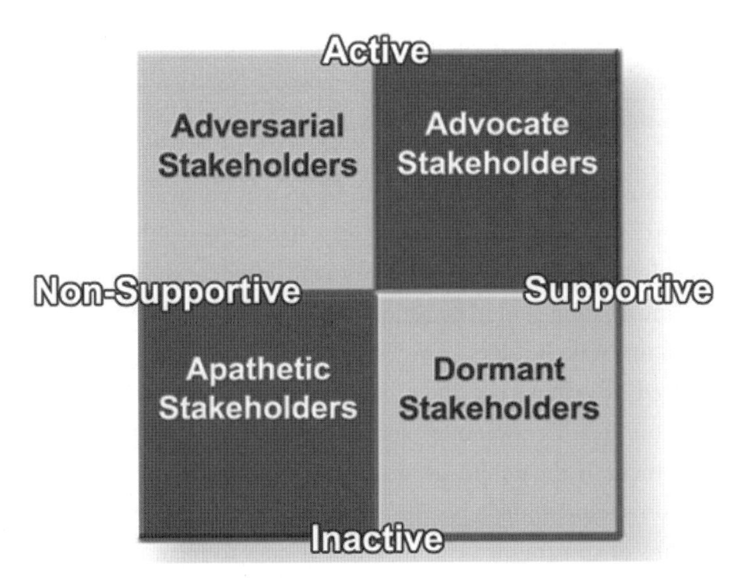

Figure 7.3. Stakeholder by communication strategy.

intervening publics, and influentials.[7] **Key publics** are those whose participation and cooperation are *required* to accomplish organizational goals. In relation to the first two steps, they are the stakeholders who have the highest priority according to their power/dependency/influence attributes, the urgency of the issue, and their level of active involvement in the issue. In Grunig's model, the key publics are called **priority publics**. To communicate effectively with these stakeholders, an organization must understand them as much as possible. Priority publics can be profiled by their demographics, lifestyles and values, media preferences, cooperative networks, and self-interests. Effective strategies appeal to the self-interests of the priority publics and reach them through the most appropriate channels (as discussed further in Chapter 9).

The **intervening publics** pass information on to the priority publics and act as opinion leaders. Sometimes these publics, such as the media, are erroneously identified as priority publics. If an organization is satisfied when the message stops at a public, then it is a *priority* public. If the expectation is that the message will be disseminated to others, it is an *intervening* public. *In most cases the media are intervening publics.* Other influentials can be important intervening publics, such as doctors who pass information on to patients, and teachers who pass information on to students. The success of many campaigns is determined by the strength of relationships with intervening publics.

Influentials can be intervening publics, but they also affect the success of public relations efforts in other ways. Influentials can either support an organization's efforts or work against them. Members of some publics will turn to opinion leaders to verify or refute messages coming from organizations. The opinion of these personal sources is much more influential than the public relations messages alone. Therefore, successful campaigns must also consider how messages will be interpreted by influentials that act as either intervening or supporting publics.

In summary, stakeholders that become active publics and that can influence the success of an organization, or can appeal to the other stakeholders with that influence, should become *priority* publics for communication strategies. Publics that are critical to getting the information to the priority publics, such as the media, need to be recognized as *intervening* publics and critical to the success of the communication strategy.

Influential groups or individuals may not be stakeholders in the organization, but may be important in shaping or framing the way the message is interpreted by the priority public, and therefore must be a part of the public relations professional's communication strategy.

A Contingency Approach to Public Relations Strategy

In order to understand how public relations should be best managed, we propose a model of contingency, mixed-motive, situational strategies based on the dimensions of (1) reactive versus proactive, and (2) self interest versus public interest. Each dimension should be seen as a continuum of more reactive/more proactive and more self-interest/more public interest rather than either/or. The interaction of these two dimensions results in four distinct approaches: defensive, responsive, assertive, and collaborative (see Figure 7.4). We will discuss each strategic approach in detail in the following pages.

Reactive Versus Proactive Dimension

Probably the two most common terms used to describe current public relations efforts are reactive and proactive. Organizations are **reactive** when they have to deal with *existing* problems that need correcting and are **proactive** when steps are taken to prevent or avert problems *before* they develop. As Liechty has noted, some public relations work is necessarily reactive because practitioners "often lack either sufficient time or freedom to respond with collaborative tactics."[8] We note that resources and the support level of the CEO might pose further constraints to public relation's ability to be collaborative.

However, organizations can take different approaches to reactive public relations, often still holding and enhancing relationships if the strategic response is carefully formulated. For example, comparing the actions of Johnson & Johnson in the Tylenol case and Exxon's response to the Valdez oil spill illustrates how companies can differ in their response to products that present a danger to their consumers. Johnson & Johnson, although victims of malicious tampering, voluntarily pulled its product from the shelves of stores in order to ensure the safety of the customer. Exxon, on

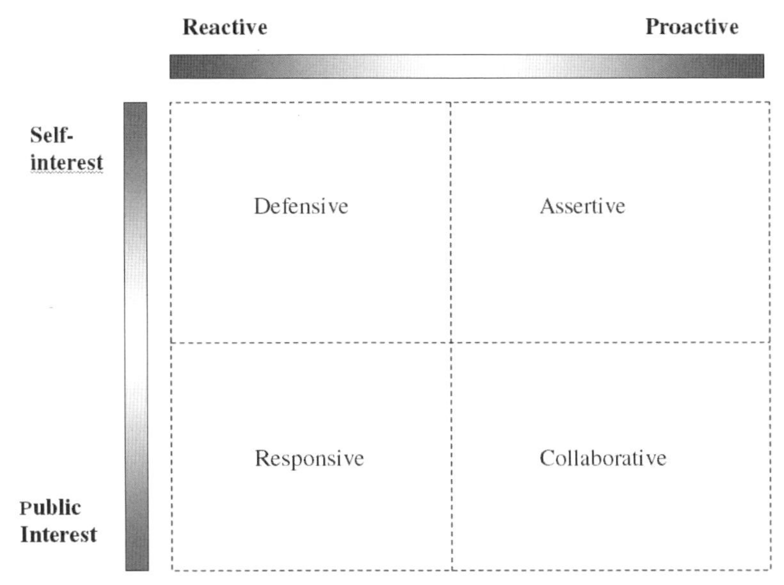

Figure 7.4. The contingency approach to public relations strategy.

the other hand, was slow to accept responsibility and to show its concern to the media and the general public. In the end, even though Exxon spent billions of dollars more than Johnson & Johnson, one came out looking like a hero while the other's reputation has become tainted as a villain to the environment. So even though both organizations had to use reactive public relations, their approaches could not have been more divergent.

Forward-thinking organizations often practice *proactive* public relations. This term means that rather than fighting change, which often proves to be a losing battle, or simply accommodating themselves to change, organizations attempt to influence change by becoming involved in the public policy process. Thus, an organization can attempt to influence public opinion with respect to specific social issues or with regard to social issues of concern to society, and attempt to influence the legislative and regulatory process with regard to specific laws and regulations.

Some organizations proactively conduct research to identify possible issues that could affect the organization and launch persuasive public information campaigns as attempts to influence public opinion and eventually the outcome of issues. Other organizations seek to collaborate with their concerned constituencies to find solutions that incorporate the interests of all parties involved and that might require change on the part of the organizations. Both of these approaches work to help prevent problems, but they use different means as preventative measures. What appears to separate how these organizations act lies in whether they are concerned primarily about their self-interests or if they also are concerned about the interests of their publics.

Self-Interest Versus Public Interest Dimension

According to the capitalist ideal, the free market economy is dependent on self-interest as a powerful motivating factor that elicits more energy and creativity than would the pursuit of someone else's interests. From a financial perspective, self-interest is defined as maximizing one's return on investment (ROI). As Buchholz explains,

> Entrepreneurs are expected to maximize profits, investors to maximize their returns in the stock market, and sellers of labor are expected to obtain the most advantageous terms to themselves. On the consumption end of the process, consumers are expected to maximize the satisfaction to themselves through their purchases of goods and services on the marketplace.[9]

Although not all social organizations have the goal of making money, even nonprofit organizations are motivated by the self-interest of survival. Therefore, *all public relations approaches will be motivated by some form of self-interest.*

Public interest is more difficult to define and defend. Fitzpatrick and Gauthier suggest that

> serving the public interest simply requires public relations professionals to consider the interests of all affected parties and make a committed effort to balance them to the extent possible while avoiding or minimizing harm and respecting all of the persons involved.[10]

Decisions are almost never made with pure self-interest or pure public interest as their motivations. Often decisions are made with collaborative interests, which allows them to "be represented as in the public interest, even if their ultimate motivation is the financial benefit of the company."[11] At the same time, Buchholz acknowledges that those in position to define the public interest can never divorce themselves from their own self-interests.

The Four Strategic Approaches Defined

The **defensive approach** is a reactive behavior that acts principally in the self-interest of the organization. The **responsive approach** is a reactive behavior that considers its impact on stakeholders. The **assertive approach** is proactive behavior that promotes self-interests in an attempt to control an organization's environment. And, the **collaborative approach** is proactive behavior that uses dialogue to create mutually beneficial solutions that incorporate the interests of both the organization and its stakeholders.

Defensive Approach

The primary form of communication for the defensive approach is planned one-way communication. The defensive approach uses the tools of publicity and public information to disseminate "facts" and "educate" publics about an organization's actions or policies in response to criticisms or crises. Sometimes a defensive approach is the only one that can be used because the organization is falsely accused of certain behaviors or standards; defending itself from such erroneous information is a legitimate and logical recourse. The defensive approach becomes a necessary response to certain situations and problems, but it is not an ideal approach if used exclusively for all situations. If public relations is relegated to practicing primarily the defensive approach in an organization, then its function is limited to damage control that results in the loss of credibility and trust with valuable publics. It is predictable that public relations professionals who are confined to practicing this approach are often representative of communication technicians and have very little power or participation in the decision-making process of an organization.

Responsive Approach

The responsive approach is also used to react to situations, but in this approach an organization acts in a fashion that demonstrates its concerns for society. This approach has become more prominent as organizations have lost the trust and confidence of their stakeholders. Social responsibility has become a rallying cry for consumer and environmental advocates. Some organizations learned that certain crises were better resolved when communication and actions showed remorse and concern toward publics and toward society. These organizations would also try to shift into a more proactive mode by identifying actions they were taking to prevent such crises in the future.

The much-documented Tylenol case set the standard for this approach. The introduction of the tamper-proof seals revolutionized product packaging. Kathie Lee Gifford's response to reports that her clothing line was using "sweatshops" is also representative of this approach. Gifford and her husband went to one of the shops with hands full of dollars to offer to the workers and pledging to campaign against sweatshops and to allow independent monitors to visit factories that made her clothes. Although skeptics could easily argue that she did this to preserve her business rather than as a response to her conscience, it is not easy to analyze motive. The responsive approach in these cases was apparently more effective than a defensive approach would have been.

Assertive Approach

Bernays's "Torches of Freedom" publicity stunt in the 1920s is a good example of the assertive approach. Bernays helped George Washington Hill and the American Tobacco Company break down the social taboo that discouraged women from smoking in public by having young debutants, or paid representations of such figures, walk in the Easter parade smoking Lucky Strike cigarettes. Using publicity and Freudian psychology of attitude change, Bernays was able to condition the marketplace to accept female smokers and thereby increase the market for Lucky Strike. Bernays played an important role in the development of this asymmetrical approach as he promoted public relations as the "engineering of consent."

Organizations that use this approach see public relations as an asymmetric strategic function that helps control the external environment.

Many corporations have used the assertive approach to shape marketing, social, and regulatory conditions that would favor them. Sometimes the assertive approach is used to the detriment of society's best interests. An example of an assertive measure that had a negative social impact is the criminal conspiracy by General Motors (GM), with Firestone Tires and Standard Oil of California, to eliminate the electric streetcar system in Los Angeles. Los Angeles had one of the best electric streetcar systems in the country before GM bought it out and converted it to GM buses that used Firestone tires and Standard Oil gasoline. In 1947 the Federal government found GM and its coconspirators guilty of criminal actions and fined them $5,000.[12] Since then, the city of Los Angeles, with support of federal grants, has spent billions of dollars on building an electric subway system to reduce pollution and public transportation problems. At the same time, there is an abundance of prosocial examples of the assertive approach, such as the civil rights movement and health awareness campaigns to reduce the risk of heart disease, cancer, diabetes, and lung diseases.

Collaborative Approach

The collaborative approach is, or should be, used by organizations when building consent and support. Collaboration relies on an organization's ability to show how its actions will benefit or not harm its stakeholders. A collaborative approach requires interaction with the publics that invites participation and involvement along the conditions of honest and genuine dialogue that respects the rights of each side and is nonmanipulative in intent or action. Collaboration emphasizes that the publics who are affected by or who can affect the action of an organization decision should participate in the decision-making process. It involves cooperation to develop equilibrium between the interests of the two parties. As Murphy noted, conflict always exists, but how the conflict is handled is usually on a continuum ranging between pure competition (a zero-sum approach) and a pure coordination approach that attempts to obtain a mutually beneficial outcome (win-win approach).[13] The collaborative approach uses the coordination motive to negotiate outcomes that will help strengthen relationships with key stakeholders, helping both an organization's self-interest and relationship maintenance.

Case: Building a Corporate Headquarters in a Prestigious Neighborhood

As an example of the collaborative approach, consider the case of a large corporation in Memphis, Tennessee, that desired to build its new headquarters in a very prestigious neighborhood. The planned site was a parklike property that the corporation owned. On the multiacre property was a large, and historical, mansion that the corporation used as an overflow office. The corporation wanted to add an additional building that would house the entire headquarters. However, this was going to be a difficult task because the city's most prominent citizens owned most of the homes in the area and recently the neighborhood had fought against converting an abandoned school building into an office and won.

Although the corporation already owned the property, it decided to collaborate with the neighborhood to find mutually satisfactory solutions rather than face a possible court injunction. The public relations director met with the homeowners association to understand the concerns and anxieties about building a corporate headquarters in the neighborhood. The major concerns were the following:

- The noise and disturbance of building the office
- The appearance of the office building
- The possibility of diminished property values, some of which exceeded a million dollars
- Other possible agitation such as increased traffic, loss of privacy, and the eyesore of an office building in their daily lives

Taking this information back to management, the public relations director worked with the CEO and other senior officers to develop strategies that would generate support for the construction of their building. Through further meetings and negotiations with the association, the corporation agreed to the following conditions:

- It would build soundproof baffles between the construction site and the neighboring homes.
- It would keep all the old-growth trees, and the office height would not exceed the height of the trees so that the building would not be visible from the homes or the adjacent streets.
- The original mansion would remain on the property with a few minor renovations.
- The new office building would be attractive even though most people wouldn't know it was there (several floors were built underground so that the office wouldn't extend above the trees, but the innovative design allowed natural light to reach the lower levels).
- A study of the community's commuter behavior showed that most residents had a half-hour drive to work. So the corporation set its hours from 7:30 a.m. to 5:30 p.m. to avoid traffic problems with its neighbors.
- To protect the sense of lost privacy that might result from customers visiting the office building, the corporation offered the neighborhood the use of its guards to watch the surrounding community for suspicious behavior.

The corporation built its new headquarters with vocal support from its neighbors and neighborhood relations were very positive for several years to come. The public relations director often posted notes from neighbors who wanted to thank a security guard for helping find a lost dog or for contributions to neighborhood fund-raising efforts to benefit charities. Using the collaborative approach, this corporation was able to achieve a win-win solution through two-way communication.

Chapter Summary

Developing positive relationships with stakeholders is a necessity for organizations. The first step is to identify your stakeholders and then prioritize them according to organizational goals and situations. A common tendency is to respond to the squeaky-wheel stakeholder. If the organization has not properly prioritized its stakeholders and their relationships, this group may get more attention than is deserved. This model demonstrates that the squeaky wheel may not be the stakeholder with the greatest priority. By using the steps outlined in this chapter, organizations can take a more systematic and comprehensive approach to prioritizing stakeholders.

To help organizations deal with varying situations, the four segment approach of the contingency model helps to create an effective public relations strategy. The understanding of these four main approaches offers you a theoretical foundation and a practical guide to practicing strategic public relations.

CHAPTER 8

Public Relations Research

The Key to Strategy

If you previously ascribed to the common misconception that public relations is a simple use of communication to persuade publics,[1] you might be surprised at the important role that research plays in public relations management.[2] We can argue that as much as three quarters of the public relations process is based on research—research, action planning, and evaluation—which are three of the four steps in the strategic management process in the RACE acronym (which stands for research, action planning, communication, and evaluation).

Importance of Research in Public Relations Management

Public relations professionals often find themselves in the position of having to convince management to fund research, or to describe the importance of research as a crucial part of a departmental or project budget. Research is an essential part of public relations management. Here is a closer look at why scholars argued that conducting both formative and evaluative research is vital in modern public relations management:

1. Research makes communication *two-way* by collecting information from publics rather than one-way, which is a simple dissemination of information. Research allows us to engage in dialogue with publics, understanding their beliefs and values, and working to build understanding on their part of the internal workings and policies of the organization. Scholars find that two-way communication is generally more effective than one-way communication, especially in instances in which the organization is heavily regulated by government or

confronts a turbulent environment in the form of changing industry trends or of activist groups.[3]

2. Research makes public relations activities *strategic* by ensuring that communication is specifically targeted to publics who want, need, or care about the information.[4] Without conducting research, public relations is based on experience or instinct, neither of which play large roles in strategic management. This type of research prevents us from wasting money on communications that are not reaching intended publics or not doing the job that we had designed them to do.
3. Research allows us to *show results*, to measure impact, and to refocus our efforts based on those numbers.[5] For example, if an initiative is not working with a certain public we can show that ineffectiveness statistically, and the communication can be redesigned or eliminated. Thus, we can direct funds toward more successful elements of the public relations initiative.

Without research, public relations would not be a true *management function*. It would not be strategic or a part of executive strategic planning, but would regress to the days of simple press agentry, following hunches and instinct to create publicity. As a true management function, public relations uses research to identify issues and engage in problem solving, to prevent and manage crises, to make organizations responsive and responsible to their publics, to create better organizational policy, and to build and maintain long-term relationships with publics. A thorough knowledge of research methods and extensive analyses of data also allow public relations practitioners a seat in the dominant coalition and a way to illustrate the value and worth of their activities. In this manner, research is the **strategic foundation** of modern public relations management.[6]

Purpose and Forms of Research

The purpose of research is to allow us to develop strategy in public relations in order to (a) conduct our campaigns with specific purpose and targeted goals, (b) operate as a part of the overall strategic management function in an organization, and (c) measure the effectiveness of public relations efforts. By conducting research before we communicate, we revise our own thinking to include the views of publics. We can segment those publics, tailor communications for unique publics, send different messages to specifically targeted publics, and build relationships by communicating with publics who have an interest in our message. This type of planning research is called **formative research** because it helps us form our public relations campaign.[7] Formative research is conducted so that we can understand what publics know, believe, or value and what they need or desire to know before we began communicating. Thereby, public relations does not waste effort or money communicating with those that have no interest in our message.

Research also allows public relations professionals to show the impact made through their communication efforts after a public relations campaign. This type of research is called **evaluation research**. Using both forms of research in public relations allows us to communicate strategically and to demonstrate our effectiveness. For example, formative research can be used to determine the percentage of publics who are aware of the organization's policy on an issue of concern. Through the use of a survey, we might find that 17% of the target public is aware of the policy. Strategically, the organization would like more members of that public to be aware of the organization's policy, so the public relations department communicates through various channels sending targeted messages.

After a predetermined amount of time, a survey practically identical to the first one is conducted. If public relations efforts were successful, the percentage of members of a public aware of the organization's policy should increase. That increase is directly attributable to the efforts of the public relations campaign. We could report, "Members of the community public aware of our new toxic waste disposal initiative increased from 17% to 33% in the last 2 months." Measures such as these are extremely common in public relations management. They may be referred to as *benchmarking* because they establish a benchmark and then measure the amount of change, similar to a before-and-after comparison.[8] The use of statistically generalizable research methods allows such comparisons to be made with a reasonable degree of confidence across various publics, geographic regions, issues, psychographics, and demographic groups.

In this section, we will provide a brief overview of the most common forms of research in public relations management and providing examples of their uses and applications and professional public relations. Building upon that basic understanding of research methods, we then return to the theme of the purpose of research and the importance of research in the public relations function.

Formal Research

Research in public relations can be formal or informal. **Formal research** normally takes place in order to generate numbers and statistics that we can use to both target communications and measure results. Formal research also is used to gain a deeper, qualitative understanding of the issue of concern, to ascertain the range of consumer responses, and to elicit in-depth opinion data. Formal research is planned research of a quantitative or qualitative nature, normally asking specific questions about topics of concern for the organization. Formal research is both *formative*, at the outset of a public relations initiative, and *evaluative*, to determine the degree of change attributable to public relations activities.

Informal Research

Informal research is collected on an ongoing basis by most public relations managers, from sources both inside and outside of their organizations. Informal research usually gathers information and opinions through conversations. It consists of asking questions, talking to members of publics or employees in the organization to find out their concerns, reading e-mails from customers or comment cards, and other informal methods, such as scanning the news and trade press. Informal research comes from the boundary spanning role of the public relations professional, meaning that he or she maintains contacts with publics external to the organization, and with internal publics. The public relations professional spends a great deal of time communicating informally with these contacts, in an open exchange of ideas and concerns. This is one way that public relations can keep abreast of changes in an industry, trends affecting the competitive marketplace, issues of discontent among the publics, the values and activities of activist groups, the innovations of competitors, and so on. Informal research methods are usually nonnumerical and are not generalizable to a larger population, but they yield a great deal of useful information. The data yielded from informal research can be used to examine or revise organizational policy, to craft messages in the phraseology of publics, to respond to trends in an industry, to include the values or priorities of publics in new initiatives, and numerous other derivations.

Types of Research

Research in public relations management requires the use of specialized terminology. The term **primary research** is used to designate when we collect unique data in normally proprietary information, firsthand and specifically relevant to a certain client or campaign.[9] Primary research, because it is unique to your organization and research questions, is often the most expensive type of data to collect. **Secondary research** refers to research that is normally a part of public domain but is applicable to our client, organization, or industry, and can be used to round out and support the conclusions drawn from our primary research.[10] Secondary research is normally accessed through the Internet or available at libraries or from industry and trade associations. Reference books, encyclopedias, and trade press publications provide a wealth of free or inexpensive secondary research. Managers often use secondary research as an exploratory base from which to decide what type of primary research needs to be conducted.

Quantitative Research

When we speak of research in public relations, we are normally referring to primary research, such as public opinion studies based on surveys and polling. (Figure 8.1 lists quantitative research methods commonly employed in public relations.) Surveys are synonymous with public opinion polls, and are one example of quantitative research. **Quantitative research** *is based on statistical generalization.* It allows us to make numerical observations such as "85% of Infiniti owners say that they would purchase an Infiniti again." Statistical observations allow us to know exactly where we need to improve relationships with certain publics, and we can then measure how much those relationships have ultimately improved (or degraded) at the end of a public relations initiative. For example, a strategic report in public relations management for the automobile maker Infiniti might include a statement such as "11% of new car buyers were familiar with the G35 all-wheel-drive option 3 months ago, and after our campaign 28% of new car buyers were familiar with this option, meaning that we created a 17% increase in awareness among the new car buyer public." Other data gathered might report on purchasing intentions, important features of a new vehicle to that public, brand reputation variables, and so on. Quantitative research allows us to have a before and after snapshot to compare the numbers in each group, therefore allowing us to say how much change was evidenced as a result of public relations' efforts.

In quantitative research, the entire public you wish to understand or make statements about is called the **population**. The population might be women over 40, Democrats, Republicans, purchasers of a competitor's product, or any other group that you would like to study. From that population, you would select a **sample** to actually contact with questions. **Probability samples** can be randomly drawn from a list of the population, which gives you the strongest statistical measures of generalizability. A **random sample** means that participants are drawn randomly and have an equal chance of being selected. You know some variants in your population exists, but a random sample should account for all opinions in that population. The larger the sample size (number of respondents), the

- Internet-based surveys
- Telephone surveys
- Mail surveys
- Content analysis (usually of media coverage)
- Comment cards and feedback forms
- Warranty cards (usually demographic information on buyers)
- Frequent shopper program tracking (purchasing data)

Figure 8.1. Methods of quantitative data collection.

smaller the margin of error and the more confident the researcher can be that the sample is an accurate reflection of the entire population.

There are also other sampling methods, known as **nonprobability samples**, that do not allow for generalization but meet the requirement of the problem or project. A **convenience sample**, for instance, is drawn from those who are convenient to study, such as having visitors to a shopping mall fill out a survey. Another approach is a **snowball sample** in which the researcher asks someone completing a survey to recommend the next potential respondent to complete the survey. A **purposive sample** is when you seek out a certain group of people. These methods allow no generalizability to the larger population, but they are often less expensive than random sample methods and still may generate the type of data that answers your research question.

Quantitative research has the major strength of allowing you to understand who your publics are, where they get their information, how many believe certain viewpoints, and which communications create the strongest resonance with their beliefs. Demographic variables are used to very specifically segment publics. Demographics are generally gender, education, race, profession, geographic location, annual household income, political affiliation, religious affiliation, and size of family or household. Once these data are collected, it is easy to spot trends by cross-tabulating the data with opinion and attitude variables. Such cross-tabulations result in very specific publics who can be targeted with future messages in the channels and the language that they prefer. For example, in conducting public relations research for a health insurance company, cross-tabulating data with survey demographics might yield a public who are White males, are highly educated and professional, live in the southeastern United States, have an annual household income above $125,000, usually vote conservatively and have some religious beliefs, have an average household size of 3.8 people, and strongly agree with the following message: "Health insurance should be an individual choice, not the responsibility of government." In that example, you would have identified a voting public to whom you could reach out for support of individualized health insurance.

Segmenting publics in this manner is an everyday occurrence in public relations management. Through their segmentation, public relations managers have an idea of who will support their organization, who will oppose the organization, and what communications—messages and values—resonate with each public. After using research to identify these groups, public relations professionals can then build relationships with them in order to conduct informal research, better understand their positions, and help to represent the values and desires of those publics in organizational decision making and policy formation.

Qualitative Research

The second major kind of research method normally used in the public relations industry is qualitative research. **Qualitative research** *generates in-depth, "quality" information that allows us to truly understand public opinion*, but it is not statistically generalizable. (Figure 8.2 lists qualitative research methods commonly employed in public relations.) Qualitative research is enormously valuable because it allows us to truly learn the experience, values, and viewpoints of our publics. It also provides ample quotes to use as evidence or illustration in our strategy documents, and sometimes even results in slogans or fodder for use in public relations' messages.

Qualitative research is particularly adept at answering questions from public relations practitioners that began "How?" or "Why?"[11] This form of research allows the researcher to ask the participants to explain their rationale for decision making, belief systems, values, thought processes, and so on. It allows researchers to explore complicated topics to understand the meaning behind them and the meanings that participants ascribe to certain concepts. For example, a researcher might ask a participant, "What does the concept of liberty mean to you?" and get a detailed explanation. However, we would expect that explanation to vary among participants, and different concepts might be associated with liberty when asking an American versus a citizen of Iran or China. Such complex understandings are extremely helpful in integrating the values and ideas of publics into organizational strategy, as well as in crafting messages that resonate with those specific publics of different nationalities.

Public relations managers often use qualitative research to support quantitative findings. Qualitative research can be designed to understand

- In-depth interviews
- Focus groups
- Case studies
- Participant observation
- Monitoring toll-free (1-800 #) call transcripts
- Monitoring complaints by e-mail and letter

Figure 8.2. Methods of qualitative data collection.

the views of specific publics and to have them elaborate on beliefs or values that stood out in quantitative analyses. For example, if quantitative research showed a strong agreement with the particular statement, that statement could be read to focus group participants and ask them to agree or disagree with this statement and explain their rationale and thought process behind that choice. In this manner, qualitative researchers can understand complex reasoning and dilemmas in much greater detail than only through results yielded by a survey.[12]

Another reason to use qualitative research is that it can provide data that researchers did not know they needed. For instance, a focus group may take an unexpected turn and the discussion may yield statements that the researcher had not thought to include on a survey questionnaire. Sometimes unknown information or unfamiliar perspectives arise through qualitative studies that are ultimately extremely valuable to public relations' understanding of the issues impacting publics.

Qualitative research also allows for participants to speak for themselves rather than to use the terminology provided by researchers. This benefit can often yield a greater understanding that results in far more effective messages than when public relations practitioners attempt to construct views of publics based on quantitative research alone. Using the representative language of members of a certain public often allows public relations to build a more respectful relationship with that public. For instance, animal rights activists often use the term "companion animal" instead of the term "pet"—that information could be extremely important to organizations such as Purina or to the American Veterinary Medical Association.

Mixed Methods/Triangulation

Clearly, both quantitative and qualitative research have complementary and unique strengths. These two research methodologies should be used in conjunction whenever possible in public relations management so that both publics and issues can be fully understood. Using both of these research methods together is called **mixed method research**, and scholars generally agree that mixing methods yields the most reliable research results.[13] It is best to combine as many methods as is feasible to understand important issues. Combining multiple focus groups from various cities with interviews of important leaders and a quantitative survey of publics is an example of mixed method research because it includes both quantitative and qualitative methodology. Using two or more methods of study is sometimes called **triangulation**, meaning using multiple research methods to triangulate upon the underlying truth of how publics view an issue.[14]

Chapter Summary

In this chapter, we examined the vital role of research in public relations management, both in making the function strategic and in adding to its credibility as a management function. Because research comprises such a large part of the public relations process—three of the four steps in the strategic management process—we discussed the purposes and forms of commonly used research in public relations. The roles of formal and informal research were discussed, as well as the major approaches to research: quantitative (numerically based) and qualitative (in-depth based) as well as the types of types of data collection commonly used in public relations in the mixing of methods.

CHAPTER 9

The Public Relations Process—RACE

Public relations works best when it is a strategic management function. Strategic public relations is focused on achieving goals and objectives that contribute to the overall purpose and mission of an organization. To be strategic, public relations practitioners need accurate information about the situations they face, the audiences they communicate with, effectiveness of their communication efforts, and the overall impact the program has on building and maintaining relationships with critical stakeholders, without whom the organization could not fulfill its purpose. Public relations practitioners may be tempted to start with tactics—such as press releases, a blog, an event, and so on—but these first should be determined by research, to help inform the overall goals and strategies of the function, otherwise they may be wasted efforts.

Constructing the Strategic Plan for a Public Relations Campaign

This process is primarily composed of four steps: using research to define the problem or situation, developing objectives and strategies that address the situation, implementing the strategies, and then measuring the results of the public relations efforts. Sometimes acronyms, such as John Marston's RACE (research, action planning, communication, evaluation) or Jerry Hendrix's ROPE (research, objectives, programming, evaluation) are used to describe the process.[1] You'll notice that that the process always starts with research and ends with evaluation.

Although it is easier to remember such acronyms, the four steps are essentially the following:

1. Use *research* to analyze the situation facing the organization and to accurately define the problem or opportunity in such a way that the public relations efforts can successfully address the cause of the issue and not just its symptoms.
2. Develop a *strategic action plan* that addresses the issue that was analyzed in the first step. This includes having an overall goal, measurable objectives, clearly identified publics, targeted strategies, and effective tactics.
3. Execute the plan with *communication* tools and tasks that contribute to reaching the objectives.
4. Measure whether you were successful in meeting the goals using *evaluation* tools.

Step 1: Formative Research to Analyze the Situation

The first step in the process is analyzing the problem or opportunity. This involves research, either formal or informal, to gather information that best describes what is going on. Research used to understand the situation and help formulate strategies is called **formative** research.

For example, a natural gas company may be considering the route for a new pipeline. It must conduct research to understand what possible obstacles it might face. Are there any environmentally protected or sensitive regions in the area? Are there strongly organized neighborhood groups that might oppose the project? What is the overall public support for natural gas and transportation pipelines? Community relations professionals are very familiar with the NIMBY (Not In My Back Yard) sentiment. Additionally, are there acceptable alternatives to the pipeline construction? Alternative routes? Alternative drilling procedures? Alternative construction times? All of these questions should be considered before the first shovel breaks ground.

According to Cutlip, Center, and Broom, research "is the systematic gathering of information to describe and understand situations and check out assumptions about publics and public relations consequences."[2] Much of this information may already exist and may have been collected by other agencies. Research that has previously been conducted is called **secondary research**. For example, the Interstate Natural Gas Association of America has conducted surveys on public opinion and communication practices of pipeline companies. Research on NIMBY and other social behaviors is also available through a review of academic and professional literature. Secondary sources are the least expensive way to gain background knowledge.

However, you may need to conduct primary research or data you collect yourself for your purposes. You may need to conduct interviews or focus groups with neighborhood associations or environmental groups. You might consider surveys with homeowners and business that might be located near the pipeline (see Chapter 8). There are many different methods to collect the data that is needed to fully understand the situation. Analysis of previous news stories about pipelines in this region would give you a good idea about the way this story might be framed by media. Another analysis of blogs and other social media about pipelines also would be a good idea. Again the purpose for gathering the information is to help with understanding the situation.

Using a SWOT Analysis

A very popular tool for analyzing situations is the **SWOT** (strengths, weaknesses, opportunities, threats) analysis. This breaks down a situation by looking at the internal and external factors that might be contributing to the situation before developing strategies. The internal factors are the **Strengths** and **Weaknesses** of the organization. The external factors are the **Opportunities** and **Threats** existing in the organization's environment (see Figure 9.1).

The first step is to look *internally* at the strengths and weakness of the organization. For example, the energy company may find that it has very strong relationships with members of the media, has good employee morale, is financially sound, and has a culture that values innovation. It may also find that it has weak relationships with environmental groups and neighborhood associations, has a culture that promotes confidence in its decisions (perhaps even bordering on arrogance), and has dedicated few resources in the past toward community relations. This information helps inform the possible strategies it needs to take regarding the construction of a new pipeline.

	Internal Factors	
	Strengths	Weaknesses
External Factors		
	Opportunities	Threats

Figure 9.1. SWOT analysis.

The *external* factors, opportunities and threats, are usually the reasons the organization finds itself in the situation. In the case of the energy company, it sees an opportunity to drill into a new methane gas deposit and provide that energy to its clients. To the energy company, this appears to be a win-win situation because it can continue to provide energy to meet the demand of its consumers. However, it also needs to assess the possible threats, which include probable legal actions from opposition groups that could lead to court injunctions. Other threats might include negative coverage of the project by the media, leading to a damaged reputation and lower public support for the project.

After conducting the SWOT analysis, you can couple the internal factors with the external factors to suggest possible strategies.

- *SO* strategies focus on using organizational strengths to capitalize on the external opportunities.
- *ST* strategies also use organizational strengths to counter external threats.
- *WO* strategies address and improve organizational weaknesses to be better prepared to take advantage of external opportunities.
- *WT* strategies attempt to correct organizational weaknesses to defend against external threats.

Constructing a Situation Analysis

Once enough data and information has been collected so that you really do understand the core contributing factors and not just the surface conditions, then it is time to write a two-paragraph statement that summarizes the situation. The first paragraph should redefine the situation using the data collected by your research. Highlight the insights gained through formal and informal research. The second paragraph should identify the problems, difficulties, and potential barriers to resolving the issue. These also should have been identified in the research, and the research also should help you recommend solutions to these barriers. For example, the energy company would address the opportunity to provide a new energy source to its customers using innovation and technology for efficient and effective delivery of the natural gas, asking its employees to be ambassadors to the community, and working with the media to tell the positive story of the project. It would also need to identify that previous pipeline projects have been delayed, and in some cases halted, because of the effective opposition of environmental groups and neighborhood associations, and that it needs to improve its efforts with community relations before starting the project.

From the description paragraphs, a succinct one-sentence **problem/opportunity statement** is written that cuts to the core of the situation and identifies the consequences of not dealing with the problem or opportunity. For example, for the hypothetical utility pipeline situation, because environmental and neighborhood groups have been influential in stopping pipeline projects in the past and this pipeline route is planned to go through sensitive regions, the company needs to build better relationships with the community through communication and action that will eliminate or reduce obstacles to building the pipeline.

Step 2: Strategic Action Planning

The strategic plan should be focused on resolving or capitalizing on the situation identified in the problem/opportunity statement. It begins by flipping the problem/opportunity statement into a **goal**. In the case of the energy company, the goal might be the following: "To use communication and actions that improve relationships with key members of the community in order to successfully complete a pipeline that delivers newly found methane gas to customers." Notice that there is room for change with the pipeline plans in this goal statement. The end goal is to build a pipeline, and in order to achieve this the company may need to make adjustments to the routes or construction of the pipeline. Care should be taken not to write goals that suggest that the public will do something you want them to do. Because publics cannot actually be controlled, it might set up the organization for failure. Instead, focus should be on what can be done to achieve the goal, such as communicate and act in such a way that earns the consent or endorsement of these publics.

The goal provides the direction for the strategic plan and **objectives** provide the direction of specific and measurable outcomes necessary to meet the goal. A good objective meets the following criteria: it should be an end and not a means to the end; it should be measurable; it should have a time frame; and it should identify the public for the intended outcome.[3]

- **End and not means to an end.** An objective should be an outcome that contributes to the goal. There are three possible outcomes for these objectives: cognitive (awareness, understanding, remembering), attitudinal (create attitudes, reinforce positive attitudes, change negative attitudes), and behavior (create behaviors, reinforce positive behaviors, change negative behaviors). The opposite of these outcome objectives are what Lindenmann called "Output Objectives,"[4] which are the means to an end. They include the communication efforts to reach the objectives such as placement of messages in influential media. These are actually strategies and not objectives (more on this later).
- **Measureable.** Objectives also help hold public relations professionals accountable for their efforts. Public relations should engage only in strategies and tactics that actually contribute to larger organizational goals. Measurable objectives often require a comparative number, such as 65% awareness of a product or program. An objective cannot be set to increase awareness by 20% if the current level of awareness is unknown. This is why formative research is needed to establish benchmarks. If

no such benchmark exists, then it is customary to establish a desired level, such as "increase awareness to 85%." The problem with this is that you do not know how close you are to that figure before the campaign. This might be an easy objective to achieve (if your level of awareness is already at or above 85%) or a very difficult one (if your awareness level is around 20%).

- **Time frame.** When will the objective be met? If there is no time frame specified, then it cannot be accountable.
- **Identify the public.** It is a good idea to identify overall objectives before tying them to a public. This helps to think about *which* publics are connected to the objective. However, to make an objective truly measurable it must identify a public, because different publics will be at different levels of awareness, attitudes, and behaviors. For example, the objective may be to increase attendance at employee benefits meetings. Research may find that the messages are getting clogged at middle management, which has many people who have a negative attitude about the meetings and are not encouraging employees. One objective might focus on increasing the level of awareness of employees while creating another objective focused on increasing positive attitudes of middle management. Of course, this also means that you should look into your meetings and find out how to improve them.

The objectives should advance overall business goals such as increase sales, increase share values, retain employees, improve social responsibility, or reduce litigation. They should also be written within the parameters of possible public relations outcomes. For example, this might look like a good objective:

- Increase sales of product X by 20% over the next 6 months among younger consumers (ages 18–24).

However, there are many variables that contribute to increased sales of the product that are not under the control of public relations such as price, product quality, and availability. Unless the public relations effort can be isolated to show that it was the variable that moved the needle on sales (such as positive publicity in one market that showed increases to sales while all other elements in the marketing mix remained the same), you may be setting yourself up for failure. And, if sales do increase, you will not be able to take credit for the increase because of the other important variables. You would have to share credit with marketing, quality control, and sales representatives. Public relations can contribute to this larger goal through increased awareness, improved attitudes, and possible consumer trials of the product. Provided that the product is of high quality, reasonably priced, and available to consumers, these activities should contribute to increased sales. So the following might be the reworked objective:

- Increase awareness of product X among young consumers (18–24) by 20% within the next 6 months.

Generally there is a hierarchy to the different levels of objectives. Lindenmann identified three levels of objectives: outputs, outtakes, and outcomes.[5]

As mentioned previously, **output** objectives are focused on the effectiveness of meeting strategies such as the number of placed messages in the media, the size of the audience that received the message, the percentage of positive messages that were contained in the stories, and so forth. It is helpful to measure output objectives because they provide a good indicator of how well the strategy has been implemented. However, they are not considered objectives as defined in this section because they are not ends but means to an end. For example, an output objective might read, "Place 30 stories in prominent newspapers about the product in the next 3 months." This is a means to the end of increasing awareness and could be measured by the output of the message but not the impact of the message. Therefore, output objectives should be relegated to the strategies section.

Outtake objectives are focused on increasing awareness, understanding, and retention of the key message points. It is far more important to know that the audience received the message than whether it was sent out. For example, you may send out a message in an employee newsletter that reaches 10,000 employees. You need to be more concerned on the impact that message had than the number of people it reached.

Outcome objectives are perhaps the most important, but also the most difficult to achieve. For example, let's say the public relations program is for the state highway patrol to increase awareness of the importance of seatbelt usage and the objective is to decrease the number of fatalities caused by not using a seatbelt. There is a diffusion process that occurs with adoption of this behavior. First, drivers need to be aware and understand the safety advantages of seatbelts. Next, they need to have a positive attitude about wearing seatbelts. Finally, this positive attitude will hopefully translate to increased use of seatbelts. However, because people are not always the rational beings we would like them to be, there is a declining measure of success at each level. People who know what is good for them do not always like it. "But seatbelts are uncomfortable." "What if the seatbelt traps me in the car after an accident?" "Seatbelts wrinkle my clothes." Even if someone has a positive attitude toward an issue, they may still not behave congruently with the attitude. It could be out of habit, laziness, or dysfunction. So to increase behaviors by 30%, attitude needs to increase by a higher level (50%) and awareness by an even higher level (80%).

Once the goal of the public relations program and measurable objectives have been established, it is time to turn attention to **strategies**. Strategies provide the means by which objectives are reached. There are certain elements that should be included in this step. First, *identify* what is trying to be accomplished with each public (tie the strategy to an objective). Second, *segment audiences* based on common characteristics. Third, *create* communication strategies that are focused on the self-interests of the publics. And, fourth, identify how publics will be *reached* with messages or actions.

Tie Strategy to Objective

Too often public relations programs have been primarily tactical and have skipped the strategic step of creating objectives. Public relations professionals are doers and often want to get to the action first. However, too many tactics have been executed because of tradition ("We always send out press releases") than because of strategy. What makes public relations *strategic* is having the action tied to the real needs of the organization. If you come up with a really clever tactic but it does not help meet any objectives it should be seriously reconsidered. Far too many resources often are wasted on creative tactics and fall short of addressing the needs of the issue. At the same time, brainstorming on strategies may lead to a legitimate idea that was not considered during the objectives phase, and it may require reevaluating the objectives. But if a strategy cannot be tied to an essential outcome, then it should not be executed.

Segment Audiences

All groups within publics should be differentiated based on common characteristics such as demographics, geographics, or psychographics. Demographics include variables such as gender, income, level of education, and ethnicity. Females may be connected to the issue very differently than males. College graduates may have different attitudes than high school graduates. Geographics describe your public by their location. People living within a thousand feet of a pipeline may have different attitudes toward energy companies than those who live a mile or farther from those lines. Psychographics segment your audience based on their values and lifestyles. People who are single, adventurous, drive fast cars, and spend a lot of their income on entertainment may have very different opinions about seatbelts than people who have small children, drive minivans, and invest most of their money on securities. It is important to segment your key publics because it will help you identify their self-interests. (See Chapter 7 for more information on identifying and prioritizing publics.)

Create Communication Based on Self-Interests

People pay more attention to communications that are tied to their values, needs, and goals. You should ask yourself what your publics value and care about (based on research). Knowing the demographic, geographic, and/or psychographic differences of key publics, you can create a message that connects them to your program. For example, for young adventurous drivers you may want to show how seatbelts allow them to have more fun by showing how someone on a curvy road stays snug in the seat, whereas someone without a seatbelt is sliding around and has less control. Meanwhile, a soccer mom would be more interested in seatbelt safety messages geared toward children. Once the self-interests have been identified, a primary message can be created that will give direction to the communication efforts. These can become slogans if they are clever and effective enough. The "Click it or Ticket" campaign uses the threat of police monitoring to encourage compliance. For the young adventurous drivers it might be more effective to have a message from sports adventurists such as race car drivers or stunt drivers explain how they rely on seatbelts.

Choose Communication Channels

The last element in the strategy is identifying the channel or medium through which you can reach target publics. The channels can be mass media, such as newspapers or television or radio programming. They can be transmitted by other mediated channels such as e-mail, blogs, or Twitter. They can also be town hall meetings, mediated slide shows, and face-to-face (interpersonal) communication. Sometimes the channel is a group of people, usually opinion leaders, such as teachers, scientists, doctors, or other experts. For example, if we wanted to reach parents in our seatbelt campaign, information kits could be sent to teachers to use in classrooms with students. These materials could be designed to take home and complete with parents. The messages found in these kits could be supported with billboards and radio public service announcements, reaching parents while they are driving. Usually the target audience is reached through multiple points of contact to reinforce the message.

So the following could be one strategy for the seatbelt campaign: "Appeal to young parents' concern for family safety through educational materials that require interaction between parents and their children enrolled in elementary schools." Often, there are several strategies for each public and for each objective.

The most creative element in the strategic planning stage is the **tactic**. Tactics are the specific communication *tools* and *tasks* that are used to execute the strategy. In the case of the seatbelt campaign, the tactics would be the elements found in the educational kit, such as crossword puzzles, coloring books, or interactive games. They would also be the billboards, public service announcements, Internet Web sites, social media applications, and other materials. The challenge is to create tactics that cut through the clutter of all the messages competing for the audience's attention. A great deal of brainstorming takes place during this stage to develop the most creative and clever messages, designs, and activities. However, there is also the temptation to get carried away with the creativity and lose sight of the tactics' purposes. A cardinal rule is to always evaluate your tactics within established strategies and objectives.

Step 3: Communication Implementation

The best public relations programs include both communication *and* action. The old adage "actions speak louder than words" is as true for public relations as it is for other business disciplines. Sometimes an organization needs to act, or react, before it can communicate. For example, if employees are not attending training seminars it might not be enough to try more creative and persuasive messages. The seminars might need to be more relevant and interesting for the employees providing something to communicate that might change behaviors. Organizations should not only expect stakeholders to behave in ways that benefit the organization; sometimes the organization needs to change its actions and behaviors to improve these critical relationships.

Two additional components to the public relations process usually are developed during the communication and action stage: the **planning calendar** and the **budget**. Once the tactics have been determined it is best to plan the development and execution of the tactics using a calendaring tool such as a Gantt chart (see Figure 9.2). A Gantt chart is a horizontal flow chart that provides a graphic illustration of when tasks should begin and end in comparison to all other tasks.

The costs for developing, distributing, and executing the tactics should also be determined. You might want to start with the wish list of all tactics and pare them down to those that will provide the greatest return on investment. Some tactics may fall by the wayside when you project their costs against their potential of meeting your objectives.

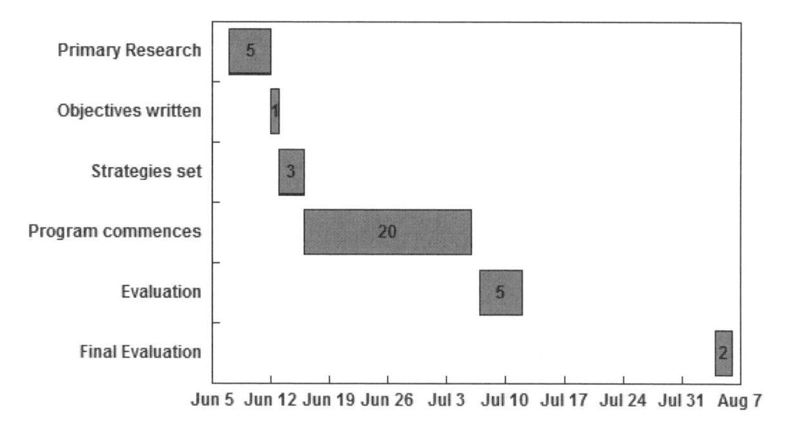

Figure 9.2. Sample Gantt chart (numbers within bars are days to accomplish task).

Step 4: Evaluation

According to Paine, four concerns should be addressed when evaluating the effectiveness of a public relations campaign:

- Define your benchmark.
- Select a measurement tool.
- Analyze data, draw actionable conclusions, and make recommendations.
- Make changes and measure again.[6]

If you have followed the steps in the public relations process then you have already identified your audiences and established objectives for each. If your objectives are measurable then you already have the criteria by which to evaluate the success of your program. If you set the objective of increasing awareness by 40% then a **benchmark has been set against which** to measure. *The benchmark compares your current situation to your past.* Paine also recommends comparing the data gathered to other organizations, such as key competitors. **Comparative analysis** makes the data much more relevant. Instead of knowing how much press coverage has been achieved; it can be compared to how much the competition is getting to determine what is called **share of voice**.

Based on this evaluation, the tools that will best help measure against stated criteria are selected. Generally, the same tools that helped establish the benchmark data are used. If primary research was used to establish benchmarks then the same methods are repeated to evaluate success. If you surveyed employees to establish awareness and attitude benchmarks, then a follow-up *survey* is the obvious measurement tool. If you used attendance at employee meetings to establish behavior benchmarks, then *counting attendance* after the public relations program is the appropriate measurement tool. As noted previously, primary research is the most expensive and requires the most expertise, but it is the best measure of the real impact of a public relations effort on stated outcome objectives, such as changes in awareness, attitudes, and behavior.

Probably the most popular evaluation tools used in public relations measure the output objectives. There are several ways to measure the effectiveness of communication output, but some are better than others. One of the earliest methods was **clip counting**. A clip is an article, broadcast story, or online message that mentions the company or product. You can either hire a clipping service or collect your own clips. At the end of a predetermined period, the number of clips obtained is examined. This measure is the most simple and convenient way to measure output and is one way to monitor media coverage. It is also the *least* informative because you do not know what the clips *mean* (they are only counted, not evaluated) except that, perhaps, it has stroked the egos of some senior management by getting their names in the media.

Many public relations measurement services will analyze media coverage to evaluate the **percentage of articles** that contain program key messages, the **prominence of the message** (for a press release, whether it was printed on page 1 versus page 16; in a broadcast, how much time was allocated to the story and where it appears in the program), the **tone of the message** (positive, neutral, negative), and how the media efforts compare with key competitors (**share of voice**). These organizations provide metrics that help establish benchmarks pertaining to program output objectives and strategies. However, to know if these communications actually affected people's awareness, understanding, attitudes, or behaviors, primary research such as surveys needs to be conducted.

Evaluation and measurement should not take place only at the end of your efforts. You should be monitoring the media constantly to determine whether your message is available for people to see (what advertisers call "reach," public relations professionals call "**opportunities-to-see**," or OTS). If the media strategy is not working, course corrections in the middle of the program are required, not after the program has been completed.

Although sophisticated measures of communication output have been developed over the years, it is still more critical to consider the outtake and outcomes of those messages. Getting the communication into various channels, be they traditional or new media, is only the means to the end of affecting attitudes, opinions, and behaviors. The outcomes need to be measured in order to tie back to organizational goals and purposes.

Cost comparisons between public relations and advertising messages are not generally used or encouraged as an evaluation tool because of the difficulty in measuring the actual impact of these messages. However, we do know that although public relations and advertising generate the same amount of product awareness, brand recall, and purchase intention, public relations content produces higher levels of product knowledge and positive product evaluation than advertising.[7]

To measure attitudes and opinions, the most popular tool remains the survey. Public opinion polls and attitude surveys can be conducted and compared to benchmarks to determine whether the messages and behaviors of an organization have had the intended effect. Intentions to behave and preferences for purchasing can also be measured through surveys, providing some figures on people's inclinations.

Behaviors can also be measured against benchmarks. Increases in employee retention, increased donations, and improved sales and investments could all be used to measure behaviors. Often the connection between communication strategy and behavioral changes could be due to other variables, so it is important to isolate and track the impact of the public relations efforts in order to evaluate whether they are the driving force in the change.

Chapter Summary

This chapter reviewed the process by which strategic public relations efforts are accomplished. The process is very structured. It suggests that formal research be conducted for formative and evaluative purposes. It requires connecting communication efforts with goals, objectives, and strategies. This process works best with planned efforts such as public relations campaigns. You may wonder how it fits for everyday tasks such as responding to a reporter's inquiry or writing a speech for an employee meeting. Because these steps are required for strategic public relations, they fit everyday duties as well. Regardless of the situation, before acting or responding the public relations professional asks, "What do I know about this situation?" (situational analysis); "What do I want to accomplish with my messages?" (goals and objectives); "How will I accomplish this with my messages?" (strategy); and "What will I say?" (tactic). This process should be ingrained if the public relations professional is to become a strategic communicator.

PART III

The Practice and Best Practices

CHAPTER 10

The Practice of Public Relations

Public relations is a large discipline that can be subdivided into many types of functions. There are four primary areas of functional responsibility or different locales in which we can categorize the profession of public relations:

1. Corporate public relations
2. Agency public relations
3. Government/public affairs
4. Nonprofit/NGO/activist public relations

These primary functional areas differ but also have the commonality of using the strategic management process. In the earlier chapter briefly outlining public relations subfunctions, we promised more specificity on how those functions actually operate within an organization. Now that we have thoroughly discussed the strategic management of public relations, we will relate how they operate in day-to-day corporate and agency settings, and how they relate to government and public affairs as well as nonprofit, NGO, and activist public relations.

Corporate Public Relations

Unlike some corporate functions, such as legal and finance, the communication function does not have as its primary mission fulfilling specific regulatory or compliance requirements. As a result, the function is rarely organized in a uniform fashion from one organization to the next. Similarly sized organizations can vary widely in the resources and number of employees devoted to communication. Reporting relationships and functional responsibilities also differ depending on the nature of the company.

For example, companies that are heavily focused on building and sustaining strong consumer brands may devote far more employees and greater attention to the communication function than organizations that operate exclusively in the business-to-business sector. A company that sells directly to consumers has a greater need for a large media relations team since it can field dozens of calls each day from both mainstream and trade media. When a new product is being launched, the staff will be called upon to plan press conferences, conduct satellite media tours with local television stations, and organize customer events.

Companies that sell their products to other businesses rather than directly to consumers may have similar needs from time to time, but they are usually on a much smaller scale. Some industries, such as fashion, entertainment, packaged goods, and travel, place a greater emphasis on communication than those with longer selling cycles, such as construction, manufacturing, and engineering. Newer fields, such as computing, also tend to rely more on public relations and social media programs than through traditional advertising channels.

In many organizations, the senior leader of the communication team reports directly to the CEO, whereas in others, that individual may report to the head of legal, marketing, or human resources. Regardless of the specific reporting relationship, in virtually all companies, the function is responsible for communicating with the media and usually has the lead role in developing employee communication as well. Public relations activities, such as the management of corporate events, press conferences, product launches, large employee gatherings, and leadership meetings normally also are managed by the chief communications officer (CCO) and his or her team.

In some companies the function is also charged with managing investor relations—that is, communicating with the company's shareholders and financial analysts who follow and report on the company. In a publicly traded company, the investor relations function must comply with a number of securities regulations regarding the company's disclosure of its financial results. These activities involve the release of quarterly and annual financial results and providing timely information to shareholders regarding any event that meets the definition of **materiality**, an event that could have a positive or negative impact on the company's share price. In fulfilling these requirements, the investor relations function works closely with the finance and legal departments, as well as the company's outside audit firm.

Most CCOs would maintain that there is no such thing as a typical day. Some of the most important qualities of successful CCOs are flexibility, patience, analytical ability, and the ability to remain calm under pressure. All organizations face potentially damaging issues every day. The CCO must monitor these issues on an ongoing basis, much like a chef watching many simmering pots on the stove. The objective in this pursuit is not to let any of these issues boil over into full-fledged crises. This task has been made harder by the ubiquitous presence of the Internet. The Web has provided the means for unhappy customers, disgruntled employees, or disappointed shareholders to voice their concerns in a very public manner with a few computer keystrokes.

Although the corporate public relations function is extremely complex and varied by industry, what follows are a few of the main responsibilities and areas of focus for any CCO.

Responsibilities and Focus of the Chief Communications Officer

Although not every organization is newsworthy or wishes to be, most larger size organizations seek to develop ongoing relationships with local, national, and international media. These relationships facilitate the flow of information to and from the organization to publics outside its boundaries. The size of the **media relations** staff is relative to the amount of press coverage the company receives. For example, a firm with a large headquarters in a major city will probably have a more active relationship with the press than a smaller organization located in a small town. Due to their level of controversy or public interest, some industries generate more media attention than others. Organizations with highly visible chief executive officers (CEOs) also tend to attract more press interest, and many CEOs have a presence on social media forums, such as Facebook or Twitter, to facilitate public interest. The CCO normally has some hand in managing these communications, as well as preparing executives for major media appearances, key industry speeches, employee meetings, testifying before government entities, and participating in community events. This facet includes speechwriting, ghost writing op-eds, and rehearsing key messages for media interviews.

Many CCOs are also responsible for overseeing **internal relations** and conducting research on employee publics. Though sometimes undervalued, a company's communication efforts with its own employees can yield the highest returns. Employees often feel they are the last to hear of major developments within their organizations, but the most successful organizations are now placing greater emphasis on keeping employees well informed, conducting an ongoing *dialogue* with internal publics, and incorporating their views into management policy in a symmetrical manner. Much of the focus in internal communication is now centered on the role of the first line supervisor. When that individual does a good job of communicating about issues, employees are more willing to pay attention to organizationwide initiatives.

Many corporate CCOs spend a great deal of time interacting with the chief marketing officers (CMOs), or marketing heads, of their organizations. Although the marketing function usually has primary responsibility for managing product brands, the corporate communication function normally manages the corporate or organizational brand, as well as the overall reputation of the organization for quality, customer service, and so on. This activity may include corporate advertising that speaks to the attributes and values of the entire organization rather than of a specific product or service. It also includes participation in industry coalitions, thought leadership forums, and academic panels. Recent research by Stacks and Michaelson found parity between public relations messages and advertising messages, meaning that public relations should be equally incorporated into the marketing mix alongside, rather than as subservient to, advertising.[1]

Increasingly, **key messages** must be delivered through Web-based channels since that is the source of information for a growing percentage of the audience. Most organizations also operate internationally, meaning that messages must be tailored for global audiences. The communication strategy must include adequate feedback mechanisms so that the organization knows how effectively key messages have been received and what further steps must be taken to provide informative and useful content to publics.

CCOs have the weighty responsibility of **issues management**, and that may include crisis and risk management in industries that are prone to hazards, risks, or product failure (such as the airline industry, the automotive industry, pharmaceuticals, and so on). The key to issues management is providing wise counsel to the senior team whenever major decisions are debated. Organizations face many choices in the course of business and virtually all the major ones have a communication dimension. As stated earlier, the CCO and the communication team act in many ways as representatives of the many publics who are not in the room when these decisions are made. An effective corporate communication function counsels the organization of potential risks, provides its publics a constant voice that can be heard by decision makers, and helps the organization translate strategy into action. The effective CCO has a thorough understanding of the organization's business objectives and the role of the communication function in helping meet these objectives.

The best counselors are those who take the time to listen carefully to the issues and concerns of the other functions to whom they are providing advice and the publics whose views they represent. In order to understand the position of these publics, the communication team relies on research. This research, which was covered more extensively in a previous chapter, provides the team with a better sense of how employees, customers, shareholders, and others view the organization generally, as well as specific issues that relate to the organization. Indeed, it is research that allows our decisions to be strategic rather than happenstance.

Finally, in a day-to-day environment, much of the time and attention of the CCO is focused on managing the public relations staff. Recruiting and developing the best talent, as in all corporate functions, is fundamental to building credibility within the organization and being positioned to offer the most useful counsel. CCOs are constantly seeking employees who can think critically, write and present articulately, and develop and maintain excellent personal relationships with their internal publics, as well as external publics. They can help their colleagues become better leaders by enhancing their skills in listening empathetically to employees and increasing their focus on workgroup communication.

The overriding mission of the CCO is to enhance the relationships an organization has with its publics by helping the organization make better, more informed decisions that take into account the impact and likely reaction to those decisions. The CCO uses all the tools available to accomplish this goal. In fulfilling this mission, the CCO works with his or her team to develop and distribute key messages that advance the organization's mission. Corporate communicators who understand this mission and can deliver tangible results are highly valued by the organizations they serve.

Agency Public Relations

In addition to in-house departments, most organizations—from small firms to huge global entities—work in partnership with public relations agencies to develop and implement communication programs. These agencies generate billions of dollars in revenue, employ thousands of counselors, and serve as the source of training and development for hundreds of young entrants to the field each year.

Agency Definitions

There are four major types of public relations agencies. They range from full service agencies to specialists who fill a particular organizational or client need. Further, they range from being units of larger, umbrella organizations to individually owned agencies.

Full Service Agencies

Some of the largest agencies offer a full spectrum of services, from traditional media relations and event planning to highly specialized research, training, and social media expertise. Some of these large agencies, such as Ketchum, Burson Marsteller, Weber Shandwick, Porter Novelli, and Fleishman-Hillard are part of large media conglomerates like Omnicom, WPP, and Interpublic. A number of large agencies, most notably Edelman, have remained independent.

Public Affairs Agencies

Agencies such as APCO Worldwide are recognized primarily for their expertise in public affairs. These agencies focus on developing advocacy positions for or against legislative initiatives, organizing grassroots campaigns, lobbying members of Congress and other government leaders or coaching their clients to do so, and participating in and often leading coalitions that link together like-minded members.

Strategic Counsel Services

Kekst, Sard Verbinnen, Abernathy MacGregor, and others focus specifically on what often is referred to as "strategic communication," including mergers and acquisitions, investor relations, and defending hostile takeovers. These agencies are brought in to supplement corporate staff and agencies of record when a company decides to make a major move, such as buying another company or selling a large subsidiary. They are also retained when a company is facing an unwanted takeover by another firm. It is common for both parties in hostile takeover attempts to retain competing strategic agencies. These are often waged in highly publicized battles that command the front pages of major media for days. The strategic counselors develop long-term relationships with a few key mergers and acquisitions (M&A) reporters for *The Wall Street Journal*, *New York Times*, and others, which they try to use as leverage on behalf of their clients.

Corporate Identity Services

Corporate identity specialists—Landor, FutureBrand, InterBrand, and others—develop branding strategies and programs for both organizations and brands. These agencies utilize extensive research to develop brand platforms for their clients that build on the existing perceptions of companies or their products. Their expertise includes graphic design, naming, brand engagement programs for employees, and complete identity systems.

Corporate Social Responsibility

In recent years a number of agencies have chosen to specialize in corporate philanthropy programs. They work with clients to determine areas in which they can match their areas of expertise with global human needs, such as hunger, health, the environment, and poverty. They design programs that help address these needs by utilizing the employees, technical expertise, and financial resources of their clients.

Trends in Agencies

Regardless of their particular area of focus, all of these agencies are being affected by a number of new industry trends.

According to a survey conducted by the Council of Public Relations Firms, the industry's trade association, agencies are finding that their clients are increasing their *outsourcing* practices. With pressures on profit margins intensifying, many companies find that they can better manage the ebbs and flows of communication activity by hiring an outside agency for certain communication activities in lieu of using internal staff.[2] When times are good and the needs multiply, organizations can increase the amount of agency support they receive; when times are lean they can cut back the support of outside firms.

Companies and agencies are also using more *virtual teams*, meaning teams that include the client's employees, the agency's employees, and independent contractors all working on the same project.[3] In many cases, these teams are located in different offices, cities, time zones, even continents, all connected through the Internet.

Most agencies are expected to provide strategic counsel, not just tactical solutions that involve executing programs. In order to do this effectively, the agency team must employ thorough *external research* that identifies pending issues and opportunities for the client. Their recommendations often go beyond the realm of communication, challenging the organization to consider the implications of policy changes or major operational decisions.

Regardless of how the agency-client relationship is structured, clients expect the agency to anticipate issues and provide a fresh perspective that can assist them in making critical decisions and recommendations to their CEOs and internal publics and colleagues. To do this well, the agency team must spend time conducting *internal research*—getting to know the unique aspects of their client's business. These aspects normally include competitive threats, labor relationships, legislative and regulatory constraints, and the global trends that will affect the future of the business.

Most large agencies have a *global reach*, they operate global networks, with major offices in North and South America, Europe, and Asia. Some do this with their own employees and others form partnerships and networks with independent agencies in other countries. Either way, it is increasingly important for multinational clients to be able to call upon an agency that can offer counsel throughout the world.

Agency Life Versus Corporate Life

The resumes of many practitioners often include experience in both agency and corporate positions, and many of the management responsibilities of the corporate CCO are also conducted by agency professionals. Agency professionals oftentimes build an area of expertise with long-term service for a client or within an industry, and work as expert prescribers resolving problems and crises as an outside consultant from the agency, and return to their agencies once the problem is solved.

The agency world offers the opportunity for varied assignments with multiple clients. A career path through the agency can provide opportunities in a wide range of areas, including media relations, issues management, crises management, brand building, event planning, and corporate reputation work. To some, one of the negative aspects of entry-level jobs in agencies is that they are highly focused on conducting events, publicity, and media pitching.

On the corporate side, most employees, especially at the entry level, are focused on a single industry or line of business. Since corporate departments are often smaller, the career path may be more limited, whereas agencies may have a diverse client list and numerous opportunities for travel. On the other hand, corporate communication positions can provide a more strategic focus, depending on the company. From a practical standpoint, the benefits offered in corporations are usually better for new hires, though this is not always the case.

Clearly, the line between corporate and agency roles is becoming less distinct. With the use of virtual teams increasing, clients are more focused on results than on the demarcation between the agency and the corporation. In both worlds, leaders are looking for ways to improve their value to the organization, whether they are serving internal or external clients.

Government Relations and Public Affairs

Government relations and public affairs are the types of public relations that deal with how an organization interacts with the government, with governmental regulators, and the legislative and regulatory arms of government. The government relations and public affairs are discussed together in this section; the two functions are often referred to as synonyms, but there are very minor differences. **Government relations** is the branch of public relations that helps an organization communicate with governmental publics. **Public affairs** is the type of public relations that helps an organization interact with the government, legislators, interest groups, and the media. These two functions often overlap, but government relations is often a more organization-to-government type of communication in which regulatory issues are discussed, communication directed to governmental representatives takes place, lobbying efforts directed at educating legislators are initiated, and so on. A strategic issue is any type of issue that has the potential to impact the organization, how it does business, and how it interacts with and is regulated by the government. Heath contends that "**public policy issues** are those with the potential of maturing into governmental legislation or regulation (international, federal, state, or local)."[4]

Public affairs is the external side of the function that deals more broadly with public policy issues of concern among constituents, activists, or groups who lobby the government on behalf of a certain perspective. Public affairs are often issues of public concern that involve grassroots initiatives, meaning that everyday citizens organize and create a movement in favor of a certain issue or perspective. In that case, public affairs specialists would work to resolve conflict or negotiate on behalf of an organization, working with these groups to create an inclusive solution to problems.

Public affairs specialists act as lobbyists on behalf of their organizations, and they interact with publics who are interested in lobbying the government for legislation regarding particular issues. Public affairs specialists might focus on a particular area of public policy, such as international trade agreements or exchange rates, security and terrorism, equitable wages and working conditions, the regulatory process, safely disposing of production by-products, and so on. The list of public policy issues with which an organization must contend is practically endless.

In some organizations, the governmental relations arm or public affairs unit is coupled with issues management, or it can even be the same public relations executive responsible for both roles. Issues management and public affairs are extremely close in their responsibilities, goals, and activities. Both issues management and public affairs seek to facilitate interaction between organization and the government or governments with whom it must deal, and to incorporate and update organizational policy in accordance with governmental standards. However, issues management is the larger function because it deals not only with governmental and regulatory publics but also many other types of publics. The governmental relations or public affairs function is more narrowly focused on legislative, regulatory, and lobbying issues.

Public affairs can be used in a corporate setting to interact on policy and legislation with the government, interest groups (or, as discussed in the following section, activist publics), and the media. An organization must also use public affairs to communicate about policy and procedures with investors, regulatory publics, employees, and internal publics, as well as communities and customers.[5]

Case: Horse Public Policy

Public affairs issues often center on a conflict of ethical values or rights between organizations and publics, and sometimes organizations, publics, and one or more branches of the government. An example would be the grassroots movement in the United States to protect wild horses from slaughter for human consumption in Europe and Asia. Many animal protection and rights organizations have lobbied officials on behalf of the horses, and those officials introduced legislation to make horse slaughter for human consumption illegal. According to the Associated Press, the U.S. House of Representatives voted 263 to 146 to outlaw the killing of horses for human consumption based on the active public affairs initiatives of the National Thoroughbred Racing Association and grassroots initiatives, such as "Fans of Barbaro."[6]

A sponsor of the slaughter-ban legislation, former Congressman Christopher Shays (R-CT) said, "The way a society treats its animals, particularly horses, speaks to the core values and morals of its citizens." Defenders of horse slaughter, including the meatpacking industry and its public affairs lobbyists as well as the U.S. Department of Agriculture argue that it provides an inexpensive way to dispose of these animals. "These unwanted horses are often sick, unfit or problem animals," said Rep. Collin Peterson (D-MN). Clearly, the two sides of this debate and all the businesses and organizations involved on each side are lobbying their point of view with governmental officials and also using the mass media to build public understanding and support for their position.

At the core of this debate is an ethical divergence over the value of equine life and the role of horses in America's society and history. At contest is the future of both those horses who live free in American herds and former sport or pet horses, and even stolen horses sold to the slaughter industry. Much money is at stake for the ranching and meatpacking industries, the Bureau of Land Management, the Department of Agriculture, and the resources invested in this legislation by the animal rights lobby.

Issues Management and Public Policy

A large part of public affairs is ongoing issues management, and the issues management function is often grouped within the same department or set of responsibilities as public affairs. For example, the public relations function at Johnson & Johnson is divided into several functional departments, the highest level being "public affairs and group issues."[7] In most organizations, especially in corporations, issues management and public affairs are inextricably linked. Organizations must manage public policy issues that they create as a consequence of their doing business.

Organizational policy must continually be revised and updated to reflect the current regulatory environment as well as the demands placed on it by publics.

Issues management is the process through which an organization manages its policy, and identifies potential problems, issues, or trends that could impact it in the future. The issues management process is a long-term, problem-solving function placed at the highest level of the organization through which it can adapt organizational policy and engage in the public affairs process. Issues management allows the top professional communicator to interact with government and publics, advising the CEO about the values of publics and how they enhance or detract from the organization's reputation with those publics.

Heath defines the issues management function in the following way: "Issues management is a process for establishing a platform of fact, value, and policy to guide organizational performance while deciding on the content of messages used to communicate with target publics."[8] Those target publics include key executives of the organization, legislators, government regulators, interest groups, and so on. Heath explained, "An issue is a contestable question of fact, value, or policy that affects how stakeholders grant or withhold support and seek changes through public policy."[9]

Why is issues management so important? Grunig and Repper noted that if an organization is unresponsive to the appeals of publics, they will lobby the government to regulate the organization or seek other public policy changes forced onto the organization in the public policy arena.[10] In that case, the organization loses its autonomy, meaning that key decisions are legislated and regulated rather than made by top management, often costing the organization a great deal of money or resources. Ideally, the organization would know how to best allocate its own resources and would manage issues in a more efficient and effective way than having those legislated and standardized across an industry, so maintaining its autonomy is generally the goal of issues management.

In issues management, we not only look for emerging issues that can affect our organization, but we also seek to build long-term, trusting relationships with publics, both governmental and grass roots. Heath explains how communication is used to help in the issues management process by noting that "the more that an organization meets key publics' need for information, the more likely they are to be praised rather than criticized."[11] Of course, managing the organization in a way that is ethical and does not seek to exploit publics or other groups allows the issues management function to truly contribute to organizational effectiveness: "Issues communication is best when it fosters mutual understanding that can foster trust. This communication must be two-way and collaborative."[12]

Issues management should be collaborative, based on the research that the issues manager has conducted. The research is what makes the issues management process "two-way," meaning in that it is based on understanding the view of publics by bringing input into managerial decision making from outside the organization. This research can be used to provide vital information at each stage of the strategic planning process. However, Heath notes that "communication may not suffice to reconcile the differences that lead to the struggle."[13] Thus, issues management cannot resolve all problems with communication or make all decisions mutually beneficial. It can help to incorporate the values of publics into strategic decision making whenever possible so that less resistance from those publics is evidenced, and their lobbying initiatives do not target the organization, which could lead to a loss of decisional autonomy through legislation.

Issues management is normally conducted on a continual, ongoing basis in which the manager is monitoring, researching, advising, and communicating about a number of concurrent issues at any given time. How many issues are managed will depend on the size of the organization and the turbulence of the industry in which it operates. Successful issues managers are those who hold in-depth knowledge of their industry, problem-solving ability, negotiating skill, and the analytical ability to examine the issue from numerous perspectives. Let us take a closer look at the process of conducting issues management.

In the mid-to-late 1970s, Chase posed an early and widely accepted model of issues management. That model included the following steps:

1. Issue identification
2. Issue analysis
3. Change options
4. Action program[14]

The Chase model, though easy to remember, is a bit simplistic, and others have elaborated on the steps in great detail. For example, Renfro's book on issues management summarized the process thus: "1) scanning for emerging issues, 2) researching, analyzing, and forecasting the issues, 3) prioritizing the many issues identified by the scanning and research stages, and 4) developing strategic and issue operation (or action) plans."[15] Although Renfro's model is an excellent one, we believe that Buchholz, Evans, and Wagley offered a slightly more comprehensive, six-step model for managing issues that is directly designed for the public policy needs of management.[16] (See Figure 10.1.)

Arguably, the most important phase of issues management is the **issues scanning, monitoring, and analysis phase**. If an issues manager fails to identify an emerging issue, the hope of creating a proactive plan to manage the issue diminishes. Once an issue emerges into the public policy arena, the organization loses control of defining the issue and time is of the essence in its management. Monitoring for emerging issues and predicting the future importance of issues is called **issues forecasting**. Issues forecasting is a bit like fortune telling; we can never accurately predict the future emergence of an issue with all of its nuances and the dynamic interactions of the issue with publics.

Another argument could be made that the research and analysis of an issue is the most important phase for determining priorities and how to best handle the new issue. The more research an organization can gather, the more informed its decisions should be. Still, an element of strategy exists within the collection of data, its analysis, and its interpretation into managerial policy. But as Heath cautions, "Data azre only as good as the insights of people who analyze them."[17]

A large part of government relations and public affairs is the **lobbying process** in which the research, knowledge, and policies formulated through issues management are communicated to legislative publics. This communication often takes place while educating elected officials on an organization's point of view, contribution to society, regulatory environment, and business practices. The legislative process is one in which organizations can integratively and collaboratively participate, helping to inform legislation. Oftentimes, lobbyists are hired to advocate for or against legislation that would potentially impact the organization.

1. Identify public issues and trends in public expectations
   - Scan the environment for trends and issues
   - Track trends in issues that are developing
   - Develop forecasts of trends and issues
   - Identify trends and issues of interest to the corporation
2. Evaluate their impact and set priorities
   - Assess the impacts and probability of recurrence
   - Assess the corporate resources and ability to respond
   - Prepare the issue priorities for further analysis
3. Conduct research and analysis
   - Categorize issues along relevant dimensions
   - Ensure that priority issues receive staff coverage
   - Involve functional areas where appropriate
   - Use outside sources of information
   - Develop and analyze position options
4. Develop strategy
   - Analyze position and strategy options
   - Decide on position and strategy
   - Integrate with overall business strategy
5. Implement strategy
   - Disseminate agreed-upon position and strategy
   - Develop tactics consistent with overall strategy
   - Develop alliances with external organizations
   - Link with internal and external communication networks
6. Evaluate strategy
   - Assess results (staff and management)
   - Modify implementation plans
   - Conduct additional research

Figure 10.1. The steps of issues management.

Source: Buchholz, Evans, and Wagley (1994), p. 41.

Regulatory impact, or "constraints imposed by outside groups or interests,"[18] is thought to be costly and is normally argued against by organizations that seek to maintain their autonomy in order to create more effective management.[19]

Nonprofit, NGO, and Activist Public Relations

Nonprofit or **not-for-profit** groups are those that exist in order to educate, fund research, advocate, or lobby on behalf of a public cause or initiative. Oftentimes, nonprofit groups are those with an educational mission existing on behalf of the public interest. For instance, the Cancer Research Foundation of America educates consumers about what food products to eat to increase healthiness and lessen cancer risk. Public relations efforts on behalf of nonprofits generally involve disseminating public information, persuading publics to adopt the ideas of the organization through the use of press agentry and asymmetrical public relations, and the use of symmetrical public relations to increase donor funding and governmental funding of the initiative.

Nonprofit public relations may exist for educational purposes, to promote an idea or cause, or to raise funds for research on an issue or problem. A well-known example would be the many cancer research foundations that exist to raise awareness about cancer and its risk factors, educate the public about preventive measures, lobby the government for further funding of cancer research, and occasionally provide grants for cancer study. Much of nonprofit public relations includes lobbying the government through educating legislators about the problem, ongoing research initiatives, and how the government can increase support for both funding and preventive measures. Nonprofit public relations often relies heavily on member relations, meaning that it seeks to maintain and develop relationships with supportive publics who can distribute the organization's message, and often pay a membership fee to assist in providing an operational budget for the nonprofit. Member relations is often conducted through the use of Internet Web sites, magazines, newsletters, and special events. **Fund-raising** or **development** is the final, vital part of nonprofit public relations. Development is tasked with raising funds from both large fund donors, writing grants for governmental support, and conducting fund-raising with smaller, private donors.

Nongovernmental organizations, or NGOs, are "soft-power" groups who do not hold the political appointees of governmental agencies, and do not have the profit motivation of corporations. They exist in order to carry out initiatives, such as humanitarian tasks, that governments are not willing to handle. NGOs often form around social issues or causes to act in concert with the government but not to be controlled by it, although their sovereignty is at question in some nations. The employees of NGOs are often former government workers or officials. NGOs often partner with local groups or leaders to accomplish specific initiatives. Gass and Seiter noted that "non-governmental (NGOs) also are particularly good at demonstrating goodwill" and that goodwill is a part of establishing credibility.[20] They explained, "Goodwill is much more likely to be communicated via 'soft power'"[21] such as NGOs. Examples would be groups such as Amnesty International or Human Rights Watch.

Activist groups are special interest groups that arise around an organization in order to establish some type of change around their particular issue of concern. Activist groups normally arise from a "grassroots movement," meaning that it comes from everyday citizens rather than those who work in government. That fact makes it slightly different from an NGO and oftentimes activist groups are less official in the formal structure of their organization and its nonprofit status, compared to nonprofits or NGOs. Activist groups can be small and informal, such as a local group of parents banding together to protest a school board decision, or they can be large and more organized, such as People for the Ethical Treatment of Animals.

Activist groups can differ in their purposes and reasons for existing, and in the amount of action-taking behavior that they undertake. For example, some activist groups are termed "obstructionist" because they obstruct a resolution to the problem in order to gain media notoriety for their issue and new membership. Greenpeace is an example of an obstructionist activist group.[22] Other activist groups might use more collaborative or integrative strategies of problem solving in an attempt to resolve their problems with an organization and have those changes integrated into organizational policy.

Activist groups also differ in the issue with which they are concerned, with some issues being broadly defined (such as "the environment") and other issues being very specific (such as "toxic waste runoff"). Grunig's study on activist group's issues is informative here; she found that "two out of every three activist groups were concerned with a single issue."[23] That single issue could be as specific as the impending destruction of a local, historic building. Or it could be a larger issue such as the amount of pollutants exuded from a manufacturing process.

Activist groups exert power on organizations in many forms of pressure, such as appearances at "town hall" type meetings, rallies and demonstrations, boycotts, anti–Web sites, e-mail campaigns, letter-writing campaigns, phone calls to legislators, lobbying, and events designed specifically to garner media attention. Activist groups are usually filled with young, educated, and motivated ideologues with a strong devotion to acting on behalf of their cause. These groups are normally quite effective in their efforts to have organizations integrate their values into organizational policy.

How to Respond to Activism

Organizations might attempt to "ignore" activist pressure, but that approach simply does not work because it often prolongs or exacerbates the activist group's campaign. When the organization stonewalls, activist groups normally approach elected officials and ask for the organization to be investigated, fined, and regulated. Activists also employ various forms of media that can both influence legislators and change public opinion, building support for their perspective that can be used in creating turbulence for the organization.

The most effective way that public relations can deal with activist groups is to engage them in a give-and-take or symmetrical dialogue to discover their issues of concern, values, wants, and priorities. Collaborative efforts to resolve conflict normally lessen the damage resulting from conflict for organizations; refusing to deal with activist groups protracts the dispute. The efficacy of activist groups, even very small ones, is well documented in the public relations body of knowledge. The *Excellence Study* contends that "regardless of the link of the dispute, the intensity of the conflict or the media coverage involved . . . all activist groups studied had disrupted the target organization."[24]

Integrative Decisions

Holding face-to-face meetings with activist leaders and members, brainstorming sessions, or joint "summits" tend to work well in building understanding between the organization and its activist. The activist group must also understand the organization's business model and constraints, and the requirements of the regulatory environment in which it operates. Asking for the opinion of activists on organizational policy is never a popular idea with senior management; however, it can result in novel adaptations of those ideas that provide a win-win solution to issues. Hearing and valuing the concerns of activist sometimes offers enough resolution to their dilemma for them to target less collaborative organizations. The crucial point of your response is that activists must be included rather than ignored. Using conflict resolution, negotiation skill, and symmetrical dialogue to understand the activist group helps the public relations professional incorporate their ideas into strategic decision making. A collaborative approach lessens the damage that activists cause to the reputation of the organization, as well as the amount of resources and time that must be spent on responding to activist pressure.

Activism Case: No Place for Gaddafi to Pitch His Tent

In late 2009, the leader of Libya, Col. Muammar Gaddafi, visited the United States for the purpose of addressing the United Nations (UN) general assembly. His visit to the United States led to citizen activism through which we can see many of the preceding principles of citizens acting on behalf of a cause or belief and pressuring the government to aid in their efforts. First, a brief look at the history of United States–Libya relations and specifically those with Col. Gaddafi provides important context for this case of activism. In 1979, the United States embassy in Libya was attacked by a mob and set on fire, causing the withdrawal of all U.S. government personnel.[25] Col. Gaddafi directly and publicly claimed responsibility for the 1988 terrorist bombing of Pan Am Flight 103 in which 270 people died over Scotland, including many Syracuse University students returning home from a study abroad program.[26] According to the U.S. Department of State, diplomatic relations with Libya were not reopened until 2006.[27] However, much hostility remains over the bombing of Pan Am flight 103 and Libya's other support of terrorist activities.

Col. Gaddafi is known for taking a Bedouin tent with him on foreign visits. A recent occasion in which this tent was problematic was when he requested to erect it on President Sarkozy's grounds in Paris in 2007, a move that caused consternation and reportedly "flummoxed presidential protocol service."[28] Gaddafi did erect this tent when he traveled to Belgium for official talks in 2004, and again when he visited Rome in 2009, using the tent to receive official guests. However, these European nations do not consider themselves as personally affected by the terrorist actions of Gaddafi in Libya. In terms of Grunig's situational theory of publics, discussed in Chapter 7, citizens of these European countries have lower problem recognition with Col. Gaddafi than do Americans. The *level of involvement* that Americans experience is higher than that of Europeans, both from the burning of the U.S. Embassy, severed diplomatic relations, and the Libyan terrorist downing of flight 103. High levels of both *problem recognition* and involvement, coupled with a feeling that one can personally impact the situation (known as low *constraint recognition*) all *predict* the rise of an activist public.

To further complicate matters with America, general outrage ensued when Scotland decided to release from prison the terrorist who was responsible for bombing Pan Am flight 103. The convicted terrorist, Abdelbaset al-Megrahi, was released just weeks before Gaddafi's UN address to the general assembly. Al-Megrahi received a hero's welcome upon return to Libya, while the families of many American victims watched the news stories vented their outrage in television interviews, letters to the editor, tweets, and blogs.

When Gaddafi and his associates began planning his trip to speak at the United Nations, to take place on September 22, 2009, they also began looking for a place to erect the Libyan tent. The Libyan embassy owns property in suburban New Jersey, where Gaddafi planned to stay and erect a tent. However, after public demonstrations outside the property, the town of Englewood, New Jersey, blocked Gaddafi from erecting the tent. Residents protesting Gaddafi's potential stay in the Libyan mission spoke frequently to the news media. Rabbi Boteach said, "I live right next door to the Libyan embassy. We want them to leave our neighborhood," adding that even the area's Muslims were against Gaddafi's visit.[29] Syracuse University alumni also appeared on broadcasts voicing their outrage at Gaddafi visiting the very state of that university.

Gaddafi petitioned to assemble the tent in Central Park, and New York City planning and other governmental officials also rejected that request. One news report led with the headline, "Have you got a permit for that Bedouin tent sir? Col. Gaddafi meets his match . . . New York planning officials."[30] Finding no home for the tent, the Libyan delegation resorted to subterfuge, impersonation, and using intermediaries to find a temporary place for Col. Gaddafi in the United States.

At this point, Gaddafi's delegation impersonated Dutch officials and attempted to rent space for Gaddafi's tent on the roof of a Manhattan townhouse, but that deal fell through.[31] Gaddafi used intermediaries to rent a Bedford, New York, estate owned by Donald Trump. Aerial photos taken from helicopters buzzed on the news media as the Bedouin tent was constructed on the 113 acre estate, known as "Seven Springs." As Gaddafi wound up his 90-minute address to the UN general assembly, outrage was growing in Bedford. Citizens and media began to congregate at the front gate of the estate, and media helicopters circled. Bedford town attorney Joel Sachs said a stop work order was issued on the tent just after 5 p.m., because it is illegal to build a temporary residence without a permit. The town official called the tent an "illegal structure."[32] News anchors commented on the power of citizen activists. Helicopters provided visuals of the tent being deconstructed that played across media outlets for the rest of the day.

Clearly, Gaddafi underestimated the power of activist publics operating within a representative government to prevent him from engaging in the normal activities of a dictator. The day following the stop work order on the tent, after it was taken down, work began again to build the tent.[33] However, Gaddafi did not visit the tent, as is his usual custom, to receive state visitors or other official visits. Perhaps Gaddafi had finally understood the message issued by activist publics, and governmental officials at their behest such as Congresswoman Nita Lowey, who said Gaddafi is "unwelcome throughout the New York area."[34] The battle over where Gaddafi could pitch his tent was easily won by civic activists, demonstrators, and governmental officials who acted on behalf of residents in their districts. Perhaps the case of erecting a tent is a small one, especially for a country such as Libya. It must address concerns of terrorism, human rights violations, and weapons of mass destruction, to name but a few. However, if activists can place the issue of Gaddafi's tent onto the media agenda and the agenda of elected officials, they clearly hold the power to impact his official visit to the United States.

Chapter Summary

In this chapter, we explained the typical functions of public relations for an organization. Corporate settings were discussed, along with the importance of access to and advising the dominant coalition of function managers who often sit at the management table, experience and knowledge of one's industry, and navigating the organizational structure to gather information and be able to best advise management. Agency settings were discussed, with regard to teamwork, strategic counsel, the fast-paced environment of consulting for clients, the changing dynamics of the news media in relation to social media applications such as Facebook and Twitter, and current trends affecting agencies. Government relations and public affairs were each defined and discussed for their role in the discussion and management of public policy issues. Issues management was discussed, and the six steps to effective issues management initiative were delineated. Finally, nonprofit, nongovernmental organization (NGO), and activists public relations were discussed in light of both their ability to impact public policy and how research shows that an organization should best respond to pressure from these groups. As case examples, the public policy issue and interest groups surrounding the horse slaughter for human consumption was discussed. The chapter concluded with a detailed examination of citizen activism and local government response to the United States visit of the Libyan leader Col. Muammar Gaddafi as an illustration of the power of activists to change their environment.

CHAPTER 11

Ethics, Leadership and Counseling Roles, and Moral Analyses

Beginning in the late 1990s and early 2000s, the role of ethics in business took on new meaning. Part of this was driven by business excesses that provoked the U.S. Congress to introduce and pass the Sarbanes-Oxley Act, an act in part driven by business' failure to conduct its business ethically. Public relations professionals have argued for years that ethical business practice is the key to establishing and maintaining relationships with key publics—whether they be stockholders or stakeholders. Ethical considerations in the practice of public relations have been on the forefront of public relations education for years, but because public relations practitioners had seats at the management table, they were not always taken seriously. This chapter introduces and examines ethics and its role in organizational leadership, the public relations professional's role in decision making, and what constitutes moral analysis.

Ethics

Questions of how to guide behavior and differentiate between right and wrong have intrigued mankind for thousands of years. From the ancient philosophy of Plato and Aristotle to the Enlightenment of Hume, Kant, Mill, and the theoretical approach of Jesus, Buddha, Confucius, Mohammad, and Aquinas, to modern-day philosophy, we explore the questions of right versus wrong, good versus evil, light versus darkness. Singer averred, "Ethics is about how we ought to live."[1] Given Singer's simple definition of ethics, public relations ethics is about how we *ought* to communicate. Much goes on behind that communication for the public relations professional. Issues managers must identify potential problems, research must be conducted, and both problems and potential solutions must be defined in an ethical manner. Therefore, **ethics** can be defined for public relations as *how we ought to decide, manage, and communicate.*

Ethics and Trust

Communication is *not* the ultimate goal of public relations. Our goal is building *relationships* through the use of ethical communication, listening, and strategic alliances, while collaboratively incorporating the ideas of others into organizational policy. We try to build both the means and fluency to create dialogue with our publics. If the purpose of public relations is to build relationships with publics, trust is an essential part of any ongoing relationship. Whether those publics are inside the organization, such as employees, management, administrative workers, or outside the organization, such as suppliers, distributors, retailers, consumers, communities, and governments, ethics is the linchpin that holds together relationships.

To understand the importance of ethics in relationships, imagine the following scenario. If you purchased a product from a company that advertises that it is the highest quality, you might feel exploited were you to find out that the organization sold the product knowing it was manufactured with defective components. Chances are, you would not want to have a long-term relationship with that organization, meaning that you would not become a repeat purchaser of their product. Through this simple example it becomes apparent that the ethics of an organization have a nebulous yet certain impact upon relationships with publics.

Ethical Culture

Ethics intersects with all levels of an organization. From the assembly line to middle management, ethics must play a role in decision making in order for an organization to be the most successful that it can possibly be. To be certain, much of the responsibility for ethics rests at the top of the organization, because without a vision and leadership from the top instilling the importance of ethics and the values of the organization, ethical behavior tends not to flourish. In other words, *public relations should act as the ethical conscience of the organization* by including the views of publics in decision making, but everyone in the organization must value ethics, most importantly the leaders of an organization.

This multipronged ethics function is what ethicists call "institutionalizing corporate conscience."[2] The ethics function must be a part not only of public relations but also of the corporate culture. This section will show you how to identify values, instill ethical values throughout the organization's culture, and consider and resolve ethical dilemmas.

Systems Theory Rationale for Ethics

Many entry and midlevel public relations professionals often wonder how they got into the territory of philosophy and ethical decision making. Allow us to explain the answer in terms of systems theory and you will soon understand why a working knowledge of moral philosophy is an absolute must for the public relations manager.

As a specialized field, public relations is in danger of being myopic or atomized. Laszlo explained that such specialized knowledge can form a barrier to entry and result in isolation, meaning that reality is viewed in fragments rather than holistically.[3] The contrasting view is **systems theory**, similar to biological systems or ecological systems, such as the body being comprised of a circulatory system, a nervous system, a digestive system, and so on. This organic view of systems was applied to society by the philosopher Luhmann to explain society as comprised of interdependent but somewhat autonomous social systems comprising the larger whole.[4] In organizational terms, an organization is a system comprised of smaller subsystems. Public relations is the function that communicates both among the subsystems of an organization and with its external environment, comprised of consumers and other publics. In systems theory terms, the **environment** is anything outside of the conceptual "boundary" of the organization. Those inside the boundary of the organization normally have a financial relationship with it; those in the environment can come and go across the boundary of the organization as consultants, for example, or they can exist wholly within the environment. Information freely crosses this boundary both as inputs to the organization when research is conducted, and output from the organization when it communicates with external publics.

In systems theory terms, public relations is a part of the management subsystem (see Figure 11.1). Similar to a nervous system, management is the brain of the organization and communication is used to coordinate its activities. The other subfunctions in a typical organization are occupied with their own areas of expertise, yet public relations must interact with them both in collecting data, identifying potential issues or problems, socializing new employees, and building organizational culture. These activities require an enormous amount of communication, listening, collaborative problem solving, and management skill. Public relations managers enact this internal communication function both across organizational subsystems, from management in a top-down fashion, and back to management when reporting on the internal state of affairs. Essentially, public relations acts as a communication conduit that facilitates the smooth internal operations of an organization.

Boundary Spanning and Counseling on Ethics

Public relations practitioners also span the boundary of an organization in maintaining relationships with publics in the external environment.

1. Management (coordinates and directs all other activities)
2. Disposal (marketing and sales)
3. Production (manufacturing)
4. Adaptation (research and development)
5. Maintenance (physical surroundings)

An open system is interdependent with its environment; the environment supplies many necessities of production, including labor, and the information necessary to adjust to market trends and manage the organization effectively. Closed systems are rare, as most organizations have varying degrees of interdependence with their environments, and thus, varying degrees of openness.

Figure 11.1. The organizational subsystems within systems theory.

When they cross this boundary in order to collect data, either formally or informally, they are known as "boundary spanners." Public relations managers scan the environment looking for messages of concern, and changing trends, thereby identifying problems with their publics within their industry. This process of monitoring the environment for potential issues of concern is called **environmental scanning.**[5]

By acting as boundary spanners, maintaining relationships with publics outside the organization, and collecting information from outside the organization through environmental scanning, the public relations function is perfectly situated to advise on ethical matters. Understanding the values of publics with whom the organization has relationships is enormously valuable because their ethical values can be represented in management decision making by the public relations manager. She or he is already familiar with the strategic publics in the environment of the organization, their desires, priorities, and issues with the organization. The relationships the public relations managers seek to build and maintain are a source of valuable input and information during ethical decision making because those publics can be consulted on issues important to them. The public relations manager is tasked with representing those views in top management decision-making sessions. No other organizational function is better suited to understand the needs and values of external publics than is the communication function. The legal department, no doubt, is well versed in understanding government and regulatory publics, but will have little knowledge of the values of publics extending beyond the legislative arena. Likewise, the marketing function will be knowledgeable about the values of consumers, but will have little knowledge of the values of the communities surrounding manufacturing sites. Only public relations fills this knowledge gap in terms of systems theory. By understanding and incorporating the values of publics, more ethically inclusive, diverse, pluralistic decisions can be made. These decisions result in a greater harmony between the organization and publics over time, fewer lawsuits, fewer disgruntled publics, fewer boycotts, and can prevent an expensive loss of reputation.

Ethics Counseling: Pros and Cons

One caveat to using a systems perspective to justify why public relations should act as an ethical counsel to senior management is that few public relations practitioners have actually studied ethics in a rigorous manner. Those who have studied ethics are likely to be more senior-level professionals, reporting to the top of their organization (normally the chief executive officer [CEO]), earning an above average salary, and the majority are male. This finding does not mean that younger, entry or mid-level and female professionals have less ethical reasoning ability, only that they have fewer chances in which to advise their organizations on ethical choices. Ethics study and training are encouraged as a way to remedy this problem; we will delve into moral deliberation shortly.

Is Public Relations in the Dominant Coalition?

A caveat of using public relations as an ethics counsel is that the public relations manager must have a seat at the senior management table in order to advise on these matters. The worldwide International Association of Business Communicators (IABC) study discussed later found that 30% of public relations professionals report directly to the CEO, 35% report one level below the CEO or have a dotted line (indirect) reporting relationship to the CEO. That finding is good news because it means that about 65% of public relations professionals worldwide have access to their CEOs and say they advise at least occasionally on ethical matters. However, the remaining 35% of public relations professionals reported no access to their senior management, meaning that they are not at the table when important ethical decisions are made, nor can they advise or give input on these decisions. Professionals oftentimes have little influence on policy, and the ethical decisions they must face are smaller in magnitude, often dealing with only technical aspects of the public relations function. For those, ethics study is often needed in order to advance their ascent into management.

Public Relations: Ethical Conscience Adviser

Should public relations advise on ethics? The public relations practitioners in a worldwide study reported the highest levels of agreement to these statements: "Ethical considerations are a vital part of executive decision-making" (mean 4.61 of 5.0 maximum) and "public relations practitioners should advise management on ethical matters" (mean 4.12 of 5.0 maximum).[6]

Clearly, there is agreement in the industry that management must consider ethics and that the role of ethical counsel falls on the shoulders of the public relations manager. Managers of communication need to consider two ethical roles and learn the basis of ethics to foster their ability to enact each. These two distinct ethical roles were first identified by the IABC *Business of Truth* study and also have been found in subsequent research.[7] The first role is managing the values inside the organization, including conducting ethics training. The second role is helping to analyze and deliberate ethical decisions alongside top management incorporating the knowledge of publics gained through boundary spanning. We will study each role thoroughly to prepare you for the many ethical challenges to be managed as a professional communicator.

Ethics Role 1: Organizational Values—The "Chicken Versus Egg" Dilemma

All organizations have a certain personality that scholars call organizational culture, and that culture also has values or values certain concepts above others.[8] Even a lack of concrete values *is* a value of sorts. Will organizations, particularly profit-seeking businesses, take a citizenship role in society? Or will they use society to achieve their own ends? These types of questions can help you discern the values of organizations. Looking specifically at an organization, you can assess the values it holds by reading mission statements,[9] policy documents,[10] codes of conduct, and ethics statements;[11] examining the statements of leaders[12] and its statements toward publics[13] and communities;[14] and the use of the organization's Web site as a dialogue building tool or simply as an advertisement.[15]

The reason we referred to a chicken and egg dilemma is because it is very difficult to determine whether ethical individuals drive ethical behavior or organizational culture drives ethical behavior, and which one comes first. Is it possible to turn an organization that holds little regard for ethics into an ethically exemplary one? Can ethics thrive in an organization in which the CEO cares little for such pursuits? What if the CEO exemplifies ethical leadership but takes over a historically unethical organization? Public relations is inextricably involved in questions such as these because it is responsible for communicating with internal publics, for helping to create and drive an enduring mission of the organization, and for helping foster an organizational culture that is responsible and includes the views of publics outside the organization.

The answer to the chicken and egg dilemma certainly varies according to organization and industry. However, ethicists generally hold that an organizational culture valuing ethics is more important than individuals.[16] Even the most ethically conscientious employee could not have prevented the bankruptcy of Enron.[17] One study exploring the chicken and egg dilemma concluded that an ethical organizational culture must be in place to foster and reward ethical decision making, lest an ethical individual making commendable decisions will not be encouraged or rewarded for doing so and thus cannot change the organizational culture toward the ethical.[18] In fact, organizations supportive of ethical decision making incorporate ethical debate and deliberation as a highly valued activity in their organizational culture.[19]

In order to act on this knowledge, the public relations function is responsible for helping to learn the values of the organization through conducting internal research and to refine and encourage the laudable values. Building an organizational culture focused on ethics takes much time and effort and a consistent commitment to communicate about not only the importance of organizational values but also the crucial role and decision making of ethical analyses. Contrary to what some managers believe, ethical decisions are not "easy" but come into play when many valid and competing views are present.[20] Building an organizational culture in which ethical debate is encouraged comes from delineating the organization's values, then reiterating those values consistently so that all employees know them, thereby encouraging the application of discussion of those values. Requiring ethics training at all levels of the organization is also necessary, as is insisting that leaders "walk the talk" to acting ethically and modeling ethical behavior.[21] They should evaluate employees based on their identification of ethical issues or conflicts, and reward ethical behavior. Ethics training is normally conducted by the public relations function or an internal relations specialist from the public relations department. It can take many forms, from online training to in-person retreats, to workbook modules, or discussion of case studies. The essential component of acting as a values manager for your organization is in identifying what the organization holds as a value and working to keep that concept central in all decisions throughout the organization.

For example, Johnson & Johnson's (J&J) well-publicized credo values the patients who use their products first, as their primary public. Therefore, patient-centered decisions dominate the decision-making framework when ethics are discussed at J&J. We can contrast that with an organization who values the bottom line above all other pursuits, a company who values innovation, one who values responsibility, or one who values respect. Different values of importance in the decision-making framework will result in a different organizational culture.

Through the communication outlets of internal relations such as employee Web sites, intranet, magazines, newspapers, blogs, and other communication channels, the public relations function can work to both understand the current values of internal publics and to instill the desired ethical values into the organizational culture. Ethical training programs could be used to educate employees of all levels on the values and ethical decision-making paradigm of the organization. It is important to have clarity and a vision of ethical values that is reinforced at all levels of the organization. Consistency, clarity, repetition, and a reward system in place for ethical decision making often speed the rate at which internal publics adapt to and adopt the values of the organization.[22]

Ethics Role 2: Ethical Counselor to Management

A second approach to ethics that public relations managers can take in an organization is to advise or counsel senior management on ethical decisions. The public relations counselor is perfectly situated in an organization to know the values of publics, and can help to incorporate those views of publics into strategic decisions and planning. She or he can discuss these issues with the CEO and advise him or her on how ethical decisions would impact the reputation of the organization.

Ethical decision-making paradigms and analyses are not usually necessary if there is a clear right and wrong in the situation. Ethical paradigms for moral analyses are helpful when there are two or more conflicting arguments of merit. If there are many "right" points of view then it is time to use an ethical decision-making paradigm to decide which decision alternative is most congruent with the values of the organization. The issues management team meetings can include the views of publics when the public relations professional is present to represent them in these meetings. Additionally, the public relations manager can use ethical decision-making frameworks to analyze the situation from multiple perspectives, and to advise the CEO and executive management on the morally desirable course of action.

Advising the CEO on ethics requires a number of qualifications on the part of the public relations manager. Training in ethics or moral philosophy is essential for ethical analysis, and that training can be academic or professional in nature. It is a must that the public relations manager understand the basics of moral reasoning in order to conduct thorough analyses and advise the CEO on ethics. The analysis of competing and valid decisions is a difficult, exceedingly complex pursuit. Having a public relations manager devoted to conducting these intensive analyses is sometimes the only way that a CEO can hear a countervailing point of view, as these executives are often surrounded by "yes men" who provide no critical analysis in the decision at hand. To prevent the sort of group think that often occurs in these situations, it is vital that the public relations executive be as objective as possible in the analyses of ethical decisions. Providing an objective ethical analysis to the CEO is one way that public relations adds value to the effectiveness of the organization.

Conducting Moral Analyses

As an objective decision maker, the public relations professional must have a high degree of autonomy and not be beholden to serving only the interests of the organization.[23] **Objective autonomy** requires that all the merits of each argument, from various publics or from the CEO, be considered equally. Although we know that no analysis can be purely objective, the goal of moral philosophy is to eliminate bias and strive to be as thorough and unbiased as possible.

Ways that the public relations practitioner can encourage, and further, autonomy include being a proficient boundary spanner, representing oneself as an objective, autonomous voice in strategy meetings rather than as an advocate of the organization's will, and seeking to use information collected from the publics in the organization's environment to enrich strategic decision making and organizational policy. Oftentimes, public relations practitioners report that they spent years developing a trusting but autonomous relationship with their CEOs, and that autonomy was granted on a gradual and slow basis.[24] Many public relations executives report that they had to be assertive in airing their analyses and that they were granted autonomy only after proving the credibility and accuracy of their analyses over time.[25]

The merits of each perspective, from publics and from the view of the organization, are considered according to ethical paradigms that help to judge the best or most ethical course of action. There are essentially two perspectives that are helpful in the analyses of the types of moral dilemmas common in public relations: consequentialism and deontology.

Consequentialism

As the name implies, **consequentialism** is based on the outcome or consequences of making a particular decision. If there are more positive consequences than negative consequences, the decision is determined to be ethical. One caveat of using consequentialism is obviously the limited ability we have to predict future consequences of potential actions. However, this type of decision making is common in public relations practice and is well suited for making decisions involving less complex scenarios. We will study two main branches of consequentialism: enlightened self-interest and utilitarianism.

Enlightened self-interest is a form of decision making in which the consequences of a potential decision are analyzed and preferential treatment is given to the decision makers' desires but not to the exclusion of the wishes of others. Thus, the decision is self-interested, but is said to be "enlightened" through the consideration of the consequences that decision will have on others. Enlightened self-interest is the most common decision-making framework in public relations practice in general,[26] especially at those in lower levels of responsibility or experience in the field.[27] This framework is sometimes called professional ethics, or responsible advocacy. Because of the preferential treatment of self-interest in this paradigm, many ethicists believe that it does not reach a standard of decision making that we can call moral.[28] Many times, the decisions made using enlightened self-interest become obsessively self-interested and therefore rather unenlightened.[29]

Utilitarianism advocates a standard of judging what is ethical based on how much it serves the interest of society, or advocating that which is ethical serves "the greater good for the greatest number" of people.[30] The tricky part of utilitarian reasoning is how we define "the good" so that you can make decisions furthering it for the majority. Originated by Bentham and refined by Mill, utilitarianism is a philosophy that analyzes the impact of decisions on groups of people, making it popular for use in public relations. However, we have to be careful in its implementation because it is easy to serve the interests of a majority and to forget the valid points of a minority, creating a disequilibrium in the system that would require a revision of the decision at a later date.

Utilitarians diverge over whether the specific decision (or act) or the general moral principle (or rule) should be put to the utilitarian test. The most common form of utilitarianism in public relations management is specific to the act under consideration, considering it in all of its detail, including the potential consequences arising from different decision alternatives. The option to resolving an ethical dilemma that creates the most positive outcomes and the least negative outcomes is considered to be the ethical option. Although utilitarianism is normally used to justify the sacrifice of one for the gain of many, Mill's theory holds that the ethical decision cannot result in harm to a public, even if they are small in number.[31] Therefore, the utilitarian test becomes a more stringent test than simply weighing numbers of people.

Creating decisions with the most positive outcomes comes naturally to most public relations managers. The resulting cost–benefit analysis arising from the use of a utilitarian paradigm is a frequently used approach to resolving ethical dilemmas in public relations. Christians explained that utilitarianism holds a "natural affinity today in democratic life toward determining the morally right alternative by comparing the balance of good over evil."[32] Seeking to create the most good in society with organizational decisions is a worthy goal. However, utilitarianism has a number of pitfalls that must be considered and compensated for in order to arrive at an ethical decision. The pitfall most concerning to ethicists is that utilitarianism judges outcomes based on sheer numbers rather than on moral principle. If a small public instituted a membership drive, for example, the utilitarian calculus would change the ultimate decision based upon the number of members, rather than on a changing of moral values. Complexity also poses problems for utilitarianism. Christians argued, "Practitioners [*sic*] usually find themselves confronting more than one moral claim at the same time, and asking only what produces 'the most good' is too limiting."[33] In fact, how do we decide the best course of action when there are equal amounts of goods to be produced?[34]

Utilitarianism also requires the public relations manager to be able to accurately predict the future consequences of each decision alternative. In reality, we know that few decisions can be made in which consequences are predicted with certainty. The dynamic world of publics, government regulators, communities, activist groups, and the mass media make predicting the consequences of organizational decisions that much more complicated, if not impossible. Finally, utilitarianism holds that the majority always benefits. What if a small but vocal minority has a valid point of concern with the organization? In utilitarianism, those views are dismissed in favor of the status quo, or larger public. Such a system can create a dangerous disequilibrium within the organization. The result of such a disequilibrium could be high employee turnover, outrage, lawsuits, or class action suits; negative coverage in the news media affecting the organizations reputation is then a distinct possibility.

The strength of utilitarianism is that it can be used to arrive at a relatively speedy analysis, and that benefit is particularly helpful in crisis situations (see Table 11.1 for an example of this speedy analysis). Utilitarian theory holds a particular affinity for business in a democratic society and the media's belief in the public's right to know. The use of utilitarianism as a method for analyzing ethical dilemmas serves public relations best when it is combined with another means of ethical analysis. Keeping

Table 11.1. An Example of Consequentialist Analysis
Utilitarian Analysis, Maximizing Public Interest and Greater Good

Decision option A	Good outcome versus bad outcome
Decision option B	Good outcome versus bad outcome
Decision option C	Good outcome versus bad outcome
Decision option D	Good outcome versus bad outcome
Ethical option result—aggregate	**Most good; least bad**

these caveats in mind when using a utilitarian analysis can also help the public relations practitioner be mindful of the potential problems arising from this approach.

Principles and Rights: Deontology

Deontology is a nonconsequentialist-based means of moral analysis. The moral analysis is not conducted in order to be based upon predicting future consequences; consequences are but one small consideration among many in a deontological approach. This paradigm places duty, principles, and rights as the things defined as "the good" that should be taken into account in order to make a decision ethical. Ross explained, "Whatever is ultimately good is also intrinsically good, i.e. is good apart from its consequences, or would be good even if it were quite alone."[35]

Moral principles are the underlying values that guide decisions, and are beliefs that are generally held to be true or good. Examples could be "the sacredness of life, justice, nonviolence, humanity, accountability, dignity, and peace."[36] Most rational people across various societies and cultures hold that those principles are morally good. Deontology seeks to eliminate capricious decision making by eliminating bias and holding to standards that have a universal acceptance as right or good.

Determining moral principles when conflicting perspectives are present is never an easy task. Deontology is a demanding form of moral analysis, requiring much information and the time and autonomy to thoroughly consider numerous competing perspectives. Deontology takes time and study of the philosophy in order to implement its three tests correctly, just as you are doing here. However, these drawbacks are also strengths because deontology results in very strong and enduring moral analyses.

Deontology was created by the 18th-century philosopher Kant, who used the virtue ethics of Aristotle to create a more concrete decision-making paradigm. Aristotle viewed the character of the speaker as an important part of the message and held that the power of persuasion should be held by only those of virtuous character who would not abuse that power by seeking to further anything but the truth. Along these lines, Kant imbued his philosophy with a sense of duty that is supposed to govern all moral decisions.[37] All rational human beings are equally able to reason through the duty of their decisions in a characteristic called moral autonomy by Kant; therefore, all rational beings are equal. Kant views equality as ethical, and the concept also means that everyone is equally obligated by that equality with the duty of making moral decisions.

Under that equal obligation, Kant posed three decision tests that he called the categorical imperative. These three decision tests are used to test decision alternatives under consideration to determine whether they maintain moral principle for those involved, including publics. Decisions must meet the standard of all three of the tests before they can be said to be ethical. Please see Figure 11.2 for a summary of the three decision tests or standards to be applied in a deontological analysis. A situation may have numerous alternatives to resolving an ethical dilemma in public relations; those alternatives can be put through the three tests to reveal any ethical flaws.

The first form of the categorical imperative states, "Act only on that maxim through which you can at the same time will that it should

1. Could you will the decision to become universal? That is, could you obligate everyone else to always do the same thing you are considering, even if you were on the receiving end?
2. Does the decision maintain the dignity and respect of publics, without 'using' anyone simply to accomplish organizational goals?
3. Is the decision made from a basis of good intention?

Figure 11.2. Deontology's three decision standards based on the categorical imperative obligating all people equally.

become a universal law."[38] This form of the categorical imperative tests the same universal standards as would be applied to others, if we could be on the receiving end of a decision, and is useful in public relations because it "leaves little room for subjective interpretation or self-interested decisions."[39]

Kant's second decision-making test, formula two of the categorical imperative, commands dignity and respect. Kant obligates decision makers to respect themselves, their organizations, as well as all other human beings. If the decision does not maintain the dignity and respect of the involved publics, then we know that it is not ethical.

Formula three of Kant's categorical imperative tests the intention behind making a decision. Kant wrote, "If our conduct as free agents is to have moral goodness, it must proceed solely from a good will."[40] Good intention is the only morally worthy basis for decision making in the Kantian view because it maintains autonomy and duty and prevents people from being used simply as a means to achieving an end.[41] This third categorical imperative test means that an organization must proceed out of good intent rather than from a basis of selfishness, greed or avarice, deception, falsity, and so on. Pure good intention should guide decision making in public relations ethics.

Kant's test is considered the most rigorous standard in moral philosophy. Once you have put an organization's potential decisions through these three tests, you can be certain that a decision with an affirmative answer on all three tests is ethical. Publics may still be able to disagree with the decision or policy, but it does allow the organization a comprehensive, systematic, and thorough means of making those decisions. Therefore, ethical dilemmas resolved through a deontological paradigm are more defensible, both in the media eye and to publics, than those made using other means. The defensibility arises from using a rational paradigm that does not privilege or bias self-interest, so the publics can be sure their view was considered by the organization.

Case: Home Depot's Leadership Crisis[42]

In January 2007, Home Depot was facing a leadership crisis. After months of pressure from shareholders, the company's board of directors had ousted high-profile CEO Robert Nardelli and replaced him with a much less visible executive named Frank Blake. The stylistic differences could not have been more striking. Though both Nardelli and Blake had joined Home Depot from General Electric, they seemed to come from different planets. Nardelli was regarded as a tough authoritarian manager who had shunned much of the cultural foundation of Home Depot and given a cold shoulder to its founders, Arthur Blank and Bernard Marcus.

Blake decided from early on to try to reconnect Home Depot to its roots. Whereas Nardelli and his team had enjoyed catered lunches on the top floor of the headquarters building, Blake instructed the senior executives to eat in the first floor cafeteria with everyone else, and pay for it themselves. He reached out to Blank and Marcus and asked them to serve as advisers as the company worked to reconnect with its customers.

Blake based his communication platform on two images, one called "the value wheel" and the other "the inverted pyramid" (see Figures 11.3 and 11.4).

In his talks with employees, Blake began showing the Value Wheel and Inverted Pyramid from the very first day of his tenure as CEO. The wheel portrayed Home Depot's core values and the inverted pyramid

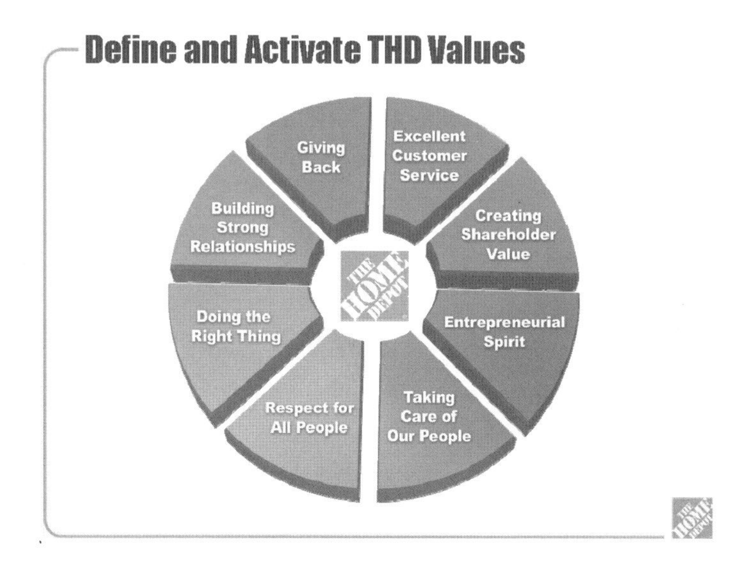

Figure 11.3. Home Depot's value wheel.

Source: Used by permission of Home Depot, Inc. (2009).

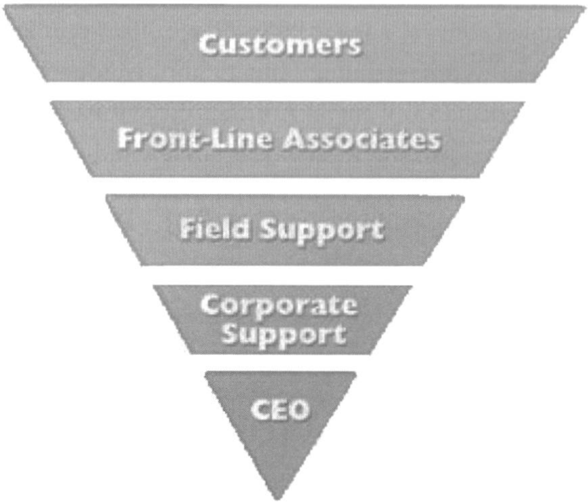

Customers
Front-Line Associates
Field Support
Corporate Support
CEO

Figure 11.4. Home Depot's inverted pyramid.

Source: Used by permission of Home Depot, Inc. (2009).

emphasized that the company's most important objective was the focus on customers and the frontline associates who directly served them.

Blake coupled this outreach to employees with some strategic decisions, as well. He made the difficult decision to spin off HD Supply, one of Nardelli's pet initiatives, and invest instead in the core retail business. At the same time, new investments were made in improving frontline customer service.

To get the message across to associates, Blake made use of some existing Home Depot channels. For example, all 300,000 Home Depot associates are required to take a monthly safety and protection quiz. The company tracks participation in this essential activity. Blake decided to use 1 minute of the quiz each month to present a brief message to all frontline associates. He also asked employees to offer suggestions on how to improve the company through an existing In-Box program. Even though headquarters receives from 300 to 400 of these ideas each week, Blake reads them all.

As Brad Shaw, Home Depot's head of communication, explained,

> We've taken our frontline associates and given them ongoing access to the CEO. Frank used to be practically unknown and now he's instantly recognized when he visits our stores. We bring in frontline folks, 20 year associates, on a regular basis and Frank meets with them to provide an opportunity to reflect on what has made HD great. We haven't changed the tools we use, we've changed the message.[43]

Shaw maintains that the message conveyed by Blake's action is really quite simple. "You have to listen to your people," he says. "The days of centralized top-down communication are over. It's a two-way communication process. Frank understands that and our frontline associates understand it. We're working to educate our management in the middle of how important this is."

Blake has emphasized the need to listen to the frontline employees particularly at the company's headquarters. When the CEO is reading the company suggestion box and spending time with frontline employees, other executives tend to follow the example. "What we're finding is that when Frank asks a question about a comment he read in the In Box, other executives want to be prepared with answers, so they're paying closer attention to the comments themselves," says Shaw.

In declaring the importance of the frontline employees, Home Depot has backed its words with definitive action. Though the company is coping with the impact of the recession along with other retailers, it had chosen to maintain the 401(k) match for employees. Unlike many of its competitors, Home Depot is continuing to grant merit increases and has paid record employee bonuses. "Other companies are fighting not to lay people off," says Shaw. "We want to stay focused on enhancing Home Depot's reputation as a good place to work."

Home Depot is also seeing positive results in terms of increases in same-store sales, which have recently been better than its primary competitor. Even though the company's gross revenues have fallen, profit in recent periods has exceeded forecasts.

Blake's primary audiences remain customers and frontline employees, but he will occasionally grant media interviews if he feels they provide an opportunity to raise the company's profile, rather than his own. "Frank is authentically humble, he doesn't want media attention but he will do it if we feel it is critically important in advancing other Home Depot messages," Shaw explains. He continued,

> He is also active in social media on his own. In some cases he will respond to blog postings on his own. He is creating a presence in social media and we don't try to control that. It is about engagement and the best way to use social media is in an unfiltered way.

In Blake's 3 years at the helm, the company has shown marked improvement in customer service. An important measure that many retailers use is called the Net Promoter Score. The company collects over 150,000 responses from customers each week and counts only positive scores about its service that rate it 9 or above on a 10-point scale. By this measure, customer satisfaction has increased over 1,000 basis points in 3 years. "The example Frank uses is that he can pick up a bottle of packaged water and there is no direct correlation between that bottle of water and the employees who packaged it. It's not easily apparent if they are happy or not," Shaw observes. "But in our case if one of our employees is unhappy you as a customer can feel it directly in the way they serve you."

The Home Depot and Frank Blake's example demonstrates the power of the chief executive officer also serving as a chief communicator to employees. In this case, it is clearly achieving results.

Chapter Summary

In this chapter, the importance of public relations as a boundary spanner who can counsel the dominant coalition on ethics and the ethical values of publics and stakeholders was emphasized. Ideally, the public relations professional should be a member of the dominant coalition who can represent the views of publics in the strategic decision making of the organization. Research on the two primary ethics roles of (a) advising on organizational values and (b) ethical counselor to management were discussed, highlighting the importance of ethical leadership and values in an organization. Means of actually conducting moral analyses in order to be a more effective ethical advisor were delineated. The moral frameworks of both consequentialism and deontology were offered as means of ethical analyses. Consequentialist analysis advises focusing on the outcomes and effect of potential decision options to maximize good outcomes and minimize bad outcomes. Deontology offered three tests through which to analyze decision options: universal duty, dignity and respect, and good intention. A case in which the role of values and ethical leadership in an organization can be seen in use in public relations and managed to help the organization achieve its goals and manage relationships was presented.

CHAPTER 12

Best Practices for Excellence in Public Relations

How do we define and measure effectiveness and excellence in public relations management? This is a crucial question to the field because it allows us to know how to help our organizations achieve their goals and to be the most effective that they can be. Studying these factors of effectiveness and excellence tells us how public relations, ideally, should be conducted in order to achieve the best results.

Effectiveness and Excellence

For more than a decade, J. Grunig and his team of researchers studied this very question as part of a nearly half-million-dollar grant from the International Association of Business Communicators (IABC). Grunig's project is called the *Excellence Study*, and the results are known as the *excellence theory*. We will review those findings here in order to help you learn how to make your public relations efforts the most effective they can be and to help your organization or clients achieve excellence.

What is organizational effectiveness? We can say that organizational effectiveness is helping any type of organization be the most efficient at what it seeks to do and the most effective it can be in accomplishing its goals and mission. Organizational effectiveness can be defined in two primary ways:

1. The strategic constituencies perspective
2. The goal attainment perspective

The **strategic constituencies perspective** holds that organizational effectiveness means that constituencies who have influence or power over the organization are at least partially satisfied with that organization. Those constituencies, such as consumers or regulatory agencies, have the power to decide whether the organization thrives or fails. When those constituencies are satisfied, an organization thrives. In this sense, organizational effectiveness means maintaining strategic relationships with constituencies that help an organization achieve its goals, such as profit, education, or continued existence.

In the **goal attainment perspective**, an organization sets clear goals that are measurable, such as rankings, market-share figures, or sales numbers. The organization knows that it has accomplished its goals when the actual figures match its stated goals. In this way, the organization is seen as effective when its stated goals are fulfilled.

An ineffective organization is termed one with "competing values" in which "the organization is unclear about its own emphases" or criteria for success.[1] This type of organization might change goals over time, have inconsistent or unclear goals, and therefore it flounders and fails to achieve effectiveness.

Organizational effectiveness involves the entire organization, not just the communication function. However, the management of communication is an important part of helping the organization as a whole achieve greater organizational effectiveness. Plus, the concepts of effective or excellent public relations can also be used to optimize the organization, structure, and management of the public relations function itself.

Grunig's *Excellence Study* identified numerous variables that contribute to organizational effectiveness. After many years of study, Grunig and the *Excellence Study*'s of researchers distilled the most important variables for public relations in making contributions to overall organizational effectiveness. These variables were distilled through both quantitative and qualitative research. The variables that emerged from the data did not vary across cultures or national boundaries, or by size of organization, or industry, therefore they were termed **generic principles of excellence**. The *Excellence Study* team identified 10 generic principles of excellent public relations:

1. Involvement of public relations in strategic management
2. Empowerment of public relations in the dominant coalition or a direct reporting relationship to senior management
3. Integrated public relations function
4. Public relations as a management function, separate from other functions
5. Public relations unit headed by a manager rather than a technician
6. Two-way symmetrical (or mixed-motive) model of public relations
7. Department with the knowledge needed to practice the managerial role in symmetrical public relations
8. Symmetrical system of internal communication
9. Diversity embodied in all roles[2]

And the team later added the last principle

10. Ethics and integrity[3]

These principles can be used to design the public relations function in an organization to structure its inner action with management and the rest of the organization, and to staff the public relations department in a way that predisposes it toward effectiveness. *The more of these factors that are present in a public relations function, the more excellent that function should be.* Another important consideration is that *the chief executive officer (CEO) must be aware of the contributions that public relations and communication in general can make toward the effectiveness of the overall organization.* He or she is probably aware of how reputation can impact the bottom line of the organization, and that reputation can be enhanced and protected by the public relations function.

Explaining the Generic Principles of Excellence

Here is a brief review of why each of the 10 generic principles of public relations is important to organizational effectiveness:

1. The involvement of public relations in the strategic management function allows for more inclusive decision making, better

organizational policy from the perspectives of publics, and more enduring decisions. Higher levels of satisfaction with the relationship are reported by publics who were considered by an organization in its strategic management process.

2. The public relations function must be empowered to report directly to the CEO in order to advise on matters involving publics, values, and ethical decision making. Although the researchers posited that a direct reporting relationship to the dominant coalition would also enhance excellence in public relations, later research found that public relations is the most excellent when reporting directly to the CEO.
3. An integrated public relations function has access to and authority in all levels and functions of the organization. It is not isolated or pigeonholed, and it is not encroached upon or subsumed by marketing or other functions, but has its own degree of autonomy.
4. It is important for public relations to be a separate management function in the organization in order to prevent encroachment by marketing or legal departments into the role and responsibilities of communication management. When these areas are usurped by other organizational functions, it is common for smaller or less strategic publics to be ignored in organizational decision making.
5. The public relations unit should always be headed by a professional public relations manager, rather than someone who is simply adept in the technical skill of writing. Managers have the research knowledge necessary to collect information, to facilitate conflict resolution, to engage in issues management, to create budgets, to resolve ethical dilemmas, and to manage the staff of the public relations department. Technicians are normally specialists in writing or other technical aspects of production, but are not normally trained in management. Without a manager in charge of the public relations function, it is likely to be pigeonholed as media relations rather than as a true management function.
6. It is important for an excellent public relations department to use the two-way symmetrical model of public relations because a dialogue-based approach has been shown more effective than any other in resolving conflicts, preventing problems, and to building and maintaining relationships with publics.

7. An excellent public relations department has the knowledge necessary to manage public relations symmetrically in that it can conduct sophisticated research to understand publics, and it can also engage in negotiation and collaborative problem solving.
8. Dialogue-based systems of internal communication are important for building teamwork, increasing employee morale and job satisfaction levels, and decreasing employee turnover. Issue research also allows issues managers to identify problems early so that they can be resolved before they escalate.
9. It is important for public relations departments to have diverse professionals in all roles of the function so that decisions and communications will be inclusive of varying viewpoints. Inclusivity breeds excellence because it lessens the feelings of alienation created by excluding or not soliciting the ideas and opinions of some publics.[4]
10. The excellence researchers added ethics and integrity as important considerations 4 years after the publication of the *Excellence Study*, remarking that ethics is important enough to be a standalone principle of excellence.[5] Bowen's research found that ethics were included in the decision making of the most successful organizations issues management, leading to higher levels of organizational effectiveness when ethics is planned, trained, and instilled throughout the organization.[6] She elaborated on ethics as the tenth generic principle of public relations, and indicated that the rational analysis of ethical dilemmas could be the most important facilitator of organizational effectiveness.[7]

How organizations measure excellence depends on the industry, the size of the organization, its goals, and whether those goals are measured through the satisfaction of strategic constituencies or through the goal attainment approach. However, the excellence study has shown that these generic principles of excellence apply to any type of organization, size of pursuit, any industry, and across cultures.

Best Practices Case: Energy Responds to Hurricane Katrina[8]

Entergy is a large-scale utility operating primarily along the Gulf Coast of the United States. In the late summer and early fall of 2005, Entergy weathered the two worst hurricanes in the company's history within the same 26-day period: Hurricanes Katrina and Rita.

The one-two punch of these powerful storms devastated the region served by Entergy. Almost 2 million homes and businesses lost power during the height of the storms' wrath. Dozens of Entergy power generation plants were forced to close, and thousands of miles of transmission and distribution lines were downed. In all, more than 1,700 structures and 28,892 utility poles were destroyed or damaged by the storms. It was devastation without precedent in modern times.

For the communication team at Entergy, the crisis caused by Katrina and Rita was more severe than any they had ever experienced. The pressure to communicate quickly with Entergy employees, customers, communities, and other publics was intense. To add to this pressure, members of the communication team had themselves suffered losses from the storms. While they grappled with how to get their jobs done, they were also trying to cope with the loss of their own homes and the impact the hurricanes had caused in their own personal lives.

Arthur Wiese Jr., Entergy's vice president of corporate communications, noted that "major storms are more than just an operational crisis for a utility company. They also pose major communications hurdles, directly impacting corporate reputation and the company's relationship with its employees, its shareholders, and its customers."

In Entergy's headquarters city, New Orleans, the damage was catastrophic. Thousands were dead or missing; tens of thousands were homeless. Electrical power was virtually nonexistent; the gas distribution system was inundated with corrosive saltwater; 1,500 displaced Entergy employees were scattered across the nation—from Los Angeles to Boston—after the company's evacuation on August 27. It was hard to know where to begin.

In the hours after the winds subsided and the scope of the damage became clear, Entergy faced multiple challenges. The company had to assemble the largest restoration workforce in its history to safely begin repairing the worst damage ever incurred to its system. To do this, Entergy had to address the logistical needs of its workers, providing a constant supply of food, water, and medication. It had to find shelter for the workforce, many of whom had lost homes. Entergy improvised a system to get workers their paychecks and to communicate with them in the absence of cell service, computers, and other traditional channels. In addition to meeting these basic human needs, Entergy needed to continue to manage its business, despite the fact that its corporate headquarters was shut down.

The communication team had actually begun preparing for Katrina long before the storm hit. As Katrina began bearing down on New Orleans, Entergy activated its system command center in Jackson, Mississippi, and moved a multidisciplinary team there on August 27, which was 2 days before Katrina made landfall. The command structure included additional transmission centers in Jackson and New Orleans, and distribution operations centers at utility operations headquarters in Louisiana, Mississippi, Texas, and Arkansas.

At these headquarters, personnel began coordinating preparation efforts, recruiting outside restoration help through mutual assistance agreements with other utilities, and lined up safe staging areas for materials and crews. Additionally, customers as well as crews in the suspected impact zone were put on alert as arrangements were being made to support the lodging of crews once the restoration began.

The company had learned some valuable lessons in the aftermath of Hurricane Ivan, which had struck its service area the previous year. Hurricane Ivan was the strongest hurricane of the 2004 Atlantic hurricane season, and it had forced Entergy to mount a full company evacuation, which had not been done before. Employees were confused about their own responsibilities during the evacuation versus those that belonged to the company. For example, Ivan demonstrated the limits on the company's ability to provide evacuation lodging, which many employees had been expecting. Through the experience with Ivan, Entergy learned how important it was to communicate clearly with employees about the differences between the company's responsibilities and the individual's responsibilities in a catastrophe.

Entergy assembled a cross-functional team in the spring of 2005 to address the lessons learned from the Ivan evacuation. The team found several key areas that posed problems for the company. The past practice of individual business units independently implementing evacuation policies resulted in chaos, including internal competition for lodging. Many employees did not fully appreciate the potential danger of a major hurricane, since the area had not experienced a direct strike in decades.

The communications team targeted these areas of confusion and implemented a new communications plan. The goal was to educate employees on the company's new evacuation policies and procedures and to provide them with information to help them prepare their own individual hurricane evacuation plans. This approach emphasized the severity of the danger posed by a major hurricane and the need to plan ahead. The company needed to explain why it was implementing more consistent storm policies, and how these changes would help Entergy's ability to implement the storm restoration plan for customers.

Communication began with supervisors, who were sent talking points and an overview of materials that would be mailed to employees in June 2005. They were also invited to attend a Webcast that provided an overview of the changes and an opportunity to ask questions. These supervisors were asked to meet with their employees within 2 weeks to explain these changes and to distribute a communications packet outlining the new procedures.

The communications team also developed a new Web site titled "IEStormNet." This Web site was designed to communicate important information before, during, and after a natural disaster. This site was made available to both employees and their families and promotional fliers were distributed that highlighted the information available through the site.

Entergy also wanted to make sure its customers were better prepared. In May 2005, Entergy constructed a corporate communications plan that aimed to help customers better appreciate the challenges it would face in restoring service in the event of a major storm. Ivan had demonstrated how difficult it would be for Entergy to restore service quickly and the company wanted customers to better understand the challenges it would face in getting them back on line. Although Ivan was a serious storm, the company had no idea at the time just how bad the 2005 hurricane season would be.

On August 29, Katrina made landfall near New Orleans. Approximately 1,500 Entergy employees were forced to evacuate. They were scattered across the nation and hard to reach since cell phone circuits were overrun and conventional telephone service was wiped out.

The company had to utilize other methods to locate, mobilize, and inform the large restoration workforce. Entergy CEO J. Wayne Leonard sent out daily e-mails to over 14,000 employees, including those unaffected by the storm. An employee information line was kept up to date with recorded messages and detailed information. The recently created IEStormNet produced daily online newsletters, which were also printed and distributed at crew staging sites. Entergy posted toll free numbers on its Web site and broadcast public service announcements on the radio asking employees to call in for information.

Maintaining employee morale during the restoration process was a major objective. Many employees had lost family members and friends to the storm. Their homes and possessions were damaged or destroyed by the winds and flood waters. These same men and women were being asked to work 18-hour shifts in hot, humid conditions, surrounded by unimaginable tragedy and destruction.

Slowly, conditions for the restoration force began to improve. By September 7, the company had set up tent cities in seven locations throughout Louisiana and Mississippi equipped with cots, food, water, and medical supplies for all of its workers. Entergy continued to pay workers until it found them jobs within the firm because it recognized the need to offer devastated employees incentives to come back to work.

Entergy CEO Leonard posted letters on IEStormNet and asked for supervisors to deliver them to crews at campsites and even in remote areas where they were working. These letters focused on the progress of the restoration efforts. In one letter, just days after Katrina hit, Leonard wrote, "Please work safely and know that this organization of caring people is working night and day to help you pull your life back together."[9]

Just days after Katrina, Entergy established the Power of Hope Fund, which aimed to help employees and customers rebuild their lives after the storms, with an initial corporate investment of $1 million. To spread news of the Power of Hope Fund, Entergy embarked on a 2-week media campaign and spread the word via television, radio, print, and the Internet. Over the period of a few months, the fund received over $4 million in donations from around the world.

Entergy also established *Operation ReSTORE Hope*. This project had both distribution centers and a virtual store where people could donate clothes, furniture, and household supplies for employees. Entergy employee volunteers and retirees staffed the distribution centers, which benefited more than 2,000 employees whose lives had been affected by the hurricanes.

The company provided redeployment coordinators in each major hub where displaced employees and their families would be relocating. These coordinators helped displaced employees and their families make a smooth transition to new work locations. They helped to provide valuable information on schools, neighborhoods, churches, local services, and resources available in the area.

Only 26 days after Katrina, just as restoration was beginning to take hold, Hurricane Rita made landfall on September 24 as a Category 3 hurricane near the mouth of the Sabine River on the Texas-Louisiana border. Rita caused even greater damage to Entergy's transmission system, severing the ties between generating plants and customers, and plunging the area from Conroe, Texas, to Jennings, Louisiana, into darkness. Over 400 substations were knocked out of service. Rita brought damaging winds to the territory of all five utility subsidiaries in the Entergy system and interrupted service to over 750,000 customers. This second storm further complicated Entergy's efforts to restore service to customers, care for the human needs of its employees, and maintain its viability as a public company.

Throughout the Katrina and Rita restoration, Entergy made every effort to maintain a mutually beneficial relationship with the media. Winning the media's support was critical to winning the support of public officials and Wall Street. Through past experience, the company had come to understand that the media's perceptions would be shaped in large measure by how well Entergy took care of its employees and customers.

Entergy used a strategy it called "One Voice" to work with the media. This strategy was effective in keeping the messages coming from all company representatives consistent and accurate during the restoration, thus minimizing any confusion about progress.

To achieve this objective, the company gave all company spokespersons, including the 45 communicators in its corporate communications department who were working on the storm restoration effort, the same sets of talking points up to four times a day to keep them informed. Entergy issued over 50 news releases and held multiple news conferences and media conference calls throughout the restoration.

Communication officials produced and managed over 40,000 radio ads, 15,000 television ads, and 700 newspaper ads. They participated in more than 300 conference calls or meetings and held dozens of coordination calls of its own to ensure the proper coordination of all messages being dispersed, both internally and externally.[10]

Reporters were looking for complete access and unique story angles regarding Entergy's restoration process. The media had been highly critical of the government's response to Katrina at the federal, state, and local levels. Entergy thus had to deal with individuals who were already skeptical of how the situation was being managed.

Using its "one voice" strategy, Entergy opened up its doors to the media. The company aggressively pushed its story with reporters and did virtually every interview that was requested. The company invited reporters to tour the command center and even to visit crews in the field. (The first to do so were from the *New York Times*, the *Associated Press*, and *USA Today*.) When Entergy used helicopters to assess the damage, a seat was usually reserved for a photographer or journalist.

Such transparency affected how the public and the government perceived Energy's restoration efforts by making available a steady flow of information to media outlets. The resulting media exposure in many cases boosted employee moral by projecting Entergy's workers as heroes.

After Katrina, Entergy New Orleans, Inc. (ENO), the smallest of Entergy's subsidiary companies, not only faced major damages to its infrastructure, but also a drastic reduction to its customer base in the city. Almost 2 months after Katrina, only 24% of Entergy's New Orleans customers had returned.

To protect its customers from drastic rate increases and to ensure continued progress in restoring power and gas service to New Orleans, Entergy

Corporation filed a voluntary petition for bankruptcy reorganization on September 23, 2005. It also asked for federal funding to alleviate its financial situation.

Entergy faced opposition from the Bush Administration when asking for this federal funding. ENO had hoped to be included in a $17.1 billion package passed by Congress in October 2005 for Katrina relief, but the request was denied. In the administration's view, federal aid for damage incurred in natural disasters rarely goes to private, for-profit companies such as Entergy. A long, bitter public struggle ensued over getting federal assistance that would enable ENO to limit rate hikes to its customers in New Orleans. By November 2006, some federal funding began to appear. However, rate hikes for ENO customers were inevitable.

When funding from the federal government was in question, Entergy made predictions in June 2006 that they would have to increase utility rates for its customers by 25%. However, by October 2006, the Louisiana Recovery Authority had approved block grants the company sought to obtain with the Chapter 11 filing. At the same time, improving conditions in the city had contributed to faster population growth. These factors led to a much more modest rate increase of 7.5%. Built into the rate increase was a plan to create a $75 million storm reserve for future hurricanes.[11]

Entergy has learned a number of lessons from the Katrina and Rita restoration that have aided in the further development of its disaster response protocol. The company better understands that employees are its most important public, surpassing even customers. If employees do not perform, company messages to other publics are diminished. Entergy has also learned that it must anticipate significant emotional strain with its employees when they are faced with such difficult personal impacts.

As a company, Entergy was reminded of the importance of having detailed operational, communications, and business continuity plans and learned that they should conduct frequent drills to test these plans. When a major storm is approaching, it is vital to get communicators to a pre-equipped command center quickly.

Entergy also learned how important it was to make its own evacuation decisions, and not rely solely on the government. In reacting to the approach of Katrina, Entergy got a head start in relocating its hurricane command center—and ultimately its whole headquarters—to Jackson,

Mississippi. This decision proved to be pivotal in allowing the restoration process to begin as quickly and effectively as possible.

Entergy also learned the value of having backup communication tactics with IEStormNet. When conventional communication systems were down, this internal Web site helped Entergy and its employees communicate much more effectively.

Finally, the company learned the importance of taking calculated risks, especially in dealing with the media. By opening its doors to the media and demonstrating the tangible steps it was taking with both employees and customers, Entergy was able to restore trust that had been damaged in the immediate aftermath of the storm. The focus on one voice, the accessibility of key executives, and the recognition that its employees were the most critical public for communication all enabled Entergy to emerge from the chaos of Katrina and Rita and regain its footing as a profitable and sustainable organization.

Chapter Summary

This chapter briefly reviewed the core knowledge of regarding what it takes to make public relations the most effective or "excellent" that it can be, based on the findings of the IABC *Excellence Study*.[12] Being excellent is contributing to organizational effectiveness, whether that effectiveness is defined through goal attainment perspectives, strategic constituency building, or continued growth and survival. The 10 principles of excellence reviewed in this chapter are said to be "generic" because they apply across cultures, industries, types of organizations, and sizes of pursuit. The more of these factors that an organization has, the more effective its public relations function should be.

Notes

Chapter 1

1. Case based on classroom lecture and interviews with Kenneth Sternad (personal communication, March 30, 2009; September 2009). Information also based on United Parcel Service (2009).

Chapter 2

1. Grunig and Hunt (1984), p. 4. Emphasis in original.
2. Public Relations Society of America (2009b).
3. Public Relations Society of America (2009a).
4. Public Relations Society of America (2009b).
5. Bowen et al. (2006).

Chapter 3

1. Grunig and Hunt (1984).
2. Cutlip (1995).
3. Grunig and Hunt (1984), p. 28.
4. Grunig and Hunt (1984), p. 29.
5. Grunig and Hunt (1984), p. 32.
6. Hiebert (1966), p. 54.

Chapter 4

1. Cutlip, Center, and Broom (2006).
2. Dozier and Broom (1995), pp. 3–26.
3. Broom and Dozier (1986), pp. 37–56.
4. Grunig, J. E. (1992).
5. *The Authentic Enterprise* (2007).
6. *The Authentic Enterprise* (2007), pp. 29–30.
7. *The Authentic Enterprise* (2007), p. 44.
8. Bowen et al. (2006).

Chapter 5

1. Grunig, J. E. (1992).
2. Grunig, Grunig, and Dozier (2002).
3. Hambrick (1981), pp. 253–276.
4. Saunders (1981), pp. 431–442.
5. Robbins (1990).
6. Grunig (1992b), p. 469.
7. Mintzberg (1980), pp. 322–341.
8. Waters and Bird (1987), pp. 15–22.
9. Sriramesh, Grunig, and Buffington (1992), pp. 577–596).
10. Weick (1969).
11. Argenti (2007).

Chapter 6

1. Griffin (2008).
2. Robbins (1990).
3. Grunig and Grunig (1992), pp. 285–326.
4. Cutlip, Center, and Broom (2006).
5. Katz and Kahn (1966); Bertalanffy (1951), pp. 303–361.
6. Buckley (1967), p. 14.
7. Pfeffer and Salancik (1978), p. 11.
8. Cutlip, Center, and Broom (2006), p. 181.
9. Robbins (1990), p. 62.
10. Robbins (1990).
11. Grunig, Grunig, and Ehling (1992), p. 68.
12. Pfeffer and Salancik (1978), p. 15.
13. Grunig, Grunig, and Ehling (1992), p. 72.
14. Carroll (1996).
15. Mitchell, Agle, and Wood (1997), pp. 853–886.

Chapter 7

1. Winn (2001), pp. 133–166.
2. Freeman (1984).
3. Grunig and Repper (1992), p. 128.
4. Dewey (1927).
5. Grunig and Hunt (1984). Grunig and Hunt developed the model based on the work of Esman (1972); Evan (1976); Parsons (1976).
6. Grunig (2005), p. 779.

7. Wilson (2005).
8. Liechty (1997), p. 48.
9. Buchholz (1989), p. 79.
10. Fitzpatrick and Gauthier (2001), p. 205.
11. Fitzpatrick and Gauthier (2001), p. 197.
12. *United States v. National City Lines, Inc., et al.*
13. Murphy (1991), pp. 115–131.

Chapter 8

1. Bowen (2003), pp. 199–214.
2. Bowen (2009a), pp. 402–410.
3. See, for example, Grunig (1984), pp. 6–29; Grunig (1992a; 2001); Grunig, Grunig, and Dozier (2002); Grunig and Repper (1992).
4. Ehling and Dozier (1992).
5. Dozier and Ehling (1992).
6. Stacks and Michaelson (in press).
7. Stacks (2002).
8. Stacks (2002); Broom and Dozier (1990).
9. Stacks (2002).
10. Stacks (2002); Stacks and Michaelson (in press).
11. Yin (1994).
12. Miles and Huberman (1994).
13. Tashakkori and Teddlie (1998).
14. See Stacks (2002); Hickson (2003).

Chapter 9

1. Marston (1979).
2. Cutlip, Center, and Broom (2006).
3. Anderson and Hadley (1999).
4. Lindenmann (2003).
5. Lindenmann (2003).
6. Paine (2007).
7. Stacks and Michaelson (2009), pp. 1–22.

Chapter 10

1. Stacks and Michaelson (2009), pp. 1–22.
2. Council of Public Relations Firms Web site (2009).
3. Council of Public Relations Firms Web site (2009).

4. Heath (1997), p. 45.
5. Lerbinger (2006).
6. The source of information for this case example is "House OKs ban on horse slaughter for meat" (2009).
7. *Hoover's Handbook of American Business* (1997).
8. Heath (1997), p. 45.
9. Heath (1997), p. 44.
10. Grunig and Repper (1992).
11. Heath (1997), p. 149.
12. Heath (1997), p. 149.
13. Heath (1997), p. ix.
14. Chase (1984).
15. Renfro (1993).
16. Buchholz, Evans, and Wagley (1994).
17. Heath (1997), p. 100.
18. Grunig, Grunig, and Ehling (1992), p. 67.
19. Mintzberg (1983).
20. Gass and Seiter (2009), p. 160.
21. Gass and Seiter (2009), p. 160.
22. Murphy and Dee (1992), pp. 3–20.
23. Grunig (1992a), p. 515.
24. Grunig (1992a), p. 523.
25. Embassy of the United States in Tripoli, Libya (n.d.).
26. Halpern (2006).
27. Embassy of the United States in Tripoli, Libya (n.d.).
28. Sage (2007).
29. Wordsworth (2009).
30. Hazleton (2009).
31. Goldman, Radia, and Berman (2009).
32. Goldman, Radia, and Berman (2009).
33. "Qaddafi Tent Back Up on Trump's N.Y. Estate" (2009).
34. "Qaddafi Tent Back Up on Trump's N.Y. Estate" (2009).

Chapter 11

1. Singer (1994), p. 3.
2. Goodpaster (2007).
3. Laszlo (1996).
4. Luhmann (1984).
5. Stoffels (1994).
6. Bowen, Heath, Lee, Painter, Agraz, McKie, et al. (2006).

7. See Bowen, Heath, Lee, Painter, Agraz, McKie, et al. (2006); Bowen (2008), pp. 271–296.
8. Goodpaster (2007); Sims and Brinkman (2003), pp. 243–256.
9. Bowen and Broom (2005).
10. Seeger (1997).
11. Murphy (1998).
12. Kidder (2005).
13. Curtin and Boynton (2001).
14. Leeper (1996), pp. 163–179.
15. Bowen (2009b, August 7).
16. Sims (1994).
17. Sims and Brinkman (2003), pp. 243–256.
18. Bowen (2000).
19. Bowen (2004b), pp. 311–324.
20. Bowen (2002), pp. 270–283; Goldberg (1993).
21. Parks (1993).
22. Goodpaster (2007).
23. Bowen (2006), pp. 330–352.
24. Bowen and Heath (2006), pp. 34–36.
25. Bowen (2009c), pp. 427–452.
26. Martinson (1994), pp. 100–108.
27. Wright (1985), pp. 51–60.
28. De George (2006).
29. Martinson (1994), pp. 100–108.
30. De George (1999), p. 57.
31. Elliott (2007), pp. 100–112.
32. Christians (2008), p. 33.
33. Christians (2008), p. 33.
34. Ross (2002).
35. Ross (2002).
36. Cooper (2009), p. 3.
37. Baron (1995).
38. Kant (1785/1964), p. 88.
39. Bowen (2004a), p. 73.
40. Kant (1963), p. 18.
41. Paton (1967).
42. Case based on interviews with Brad Shaw (personal communication, September 2009). Information also based on Home Depot, Inc. (2009).
43. Interviews with Brad Shaw (personal communication, September 2009).

Chapter 12

1. Robbins (1990), p. 77.
2. Vercic, Grunig, and Grunig (1996), pp. 37–40.
3. Vercic, Grunig, and Grunig (1996), p. 58.
4. Vercic, Grunig, and Grunig (1996), p. 58.
5. Vercic, Grunig, and Grunig (1996), p. 58.
6. Bowen (2004b), pp. 311–324.
7. Bowen (2004b), pp. 311–324.
8. Case based on Entergy company documents and interviews with Art Wiese (personal communication, 2009). Information also based on Entergy's (2009) corporate Web site, http://www.entergy.com
9. IEStormNet Update. Entergy New Orleans and city council agree to modest, phased-in rate plan (2006, October 27).
10. Entergy, Hurricanes Katrina and Rita Final Executive Summary Report (2005, October 18).
11. IEStormNet Update. Entergy New Orleans and city council agree to modest, phased-in rate plan (2006, October 27).
12. Grunig, J. E. (1992).

References

Anderson, F., & Hadley, L. (1999). *Guidelines for setting measurable public relations objectives*. Institute for Public Relations, retrieved February 6, 2010, from http://www.instituteforpr.org/ipr_info/measureable_public_objectives

Argenti, P. (2007). *Corporate communication* (4th ed.). Boston: McGraw-Hill/Irwin.

The Authentic Enterprise. (2007). New York: Arthur W. Page Society.

Baron, M. W. (1995). *Kantian ethics almost without apology*. Ithaca, NY: Cornell University Press.

Bertalanffy, L. von. (1951). General system theory: A new approach to unity of science. *Human Biology, 23*, 303–361.

Bowen, S. A. (2000). *Is ethical public relations ingrained in organizational culture or is it the domain of individual practitioners*? Paper presented at the meeting of the Public Relations Society of America Educators Academy, Communication Sciences Division, Miami, Florida.

Bowen, S. A. (2002). Elite executives in issues management: The role of ethical paradigms in decision making. *Journal of Public Affairs, 2*, 270–283.

Bowen, S. A. (2003). "I thought it would be more glamorous": Preconceptions and misconceptions of public relations among students in the principles course. *Public Relations Review, 29*, 199–214.

Bowen, S. A. (2004a). Expansion of ethics as the tenth generic principle of public relations excellence: A Kantian theory and model for managing ethical issues. *Journal of Public Relations Research, 16*, 65–92.

Bowen, S. A. (2004b). Organizational factors encouraging ethical decision making: An exploration into the case of an exemplar. *Journal of Business Ethics, 52*, 311–324.

Bowen, S. A. (2006). Autonomy in communication: Inclusion in strategic management and ethical decision-making, a comparative case analysis. *Journal of Communication Management, 10*, 330–352.

Bowen, S. A. (2008). A state of neglect: Public relations as "corporate conscience" or ethics counsel. *Journal of Public Relations Research, 20*, 271–296.

Bowen, S. A. (2009a). All glamour, no substance? How public relations majors and potential majors in an exemplar program view the industry and function. *Public Relations Review, 35*, 402–410.

Bowen, S. A. (2009b, August 7). *Applied ethics and stakeholder management on corporate websites.* Paper presented at the meeting of the Association for Education in Journalism and Mass Communication, Boston, MA.

Bowen, S. A. (2009c). What communication professionals tell us regarding dominant coalition access and gaining membership. *Journal of Applied Communication Research, 37*, 427–452.

Bowen, S. A., & Broom, G. M. (2005). Internal relations and employee communication. In S. M. Cutlip, A. H. Center & G. M. Broom (Eds.), *Effective public relations* (Chapter 9). Upper Saddle River, NJ: Pearson Prentice Hall.

Bowen, S. A., & Heath, R. L. (2006). Under the microscope: Ethics in business. *Communication World, 23*, 34–36.

Bowen, S. A., Heath, R. L., Lee, J., Painter, G., Agraz, F. J., McKie, D., et al. (2006). *The business of truth: A guide to ethical communication.* San Francisco, CA: International Association of Business Communicators.

Broom, G. M., & Dozier, D. M. (1986). Advancement for public relations role models. *Public Relations Review, 12*, 37–56.

Broom, G., & Dozier, D. (1990). *Using research in public relations: Applications to program management.* Englewood Cliffs, NJ: Prentice Hall.

Buchholz, R. A. (1989). *Business Environment and Public Policy.* Englewood Cliffs, NJ: Prentice Hall.

Buchholz, R. A., Evans, W. D., & Wagley, R. A. (1994). *Management responses to public issues: Concepts and cases in strategy formulation* (3rd ed.). Upper Saddle River, NJ: Prentice Hall.

Buckley, W. (1967). *Sociology and modern systems theory.* Englewood Cliffs, NJ: Prentice Hall.

Carroll, A. B. (1996). *Business & Society: Ethics and Stakeholder Management.* Cincinnati, OH: Southwestern College Publishing.

Chase, W. H. (1984). *Issue management: Origins of the future.* Stamford, CT: Issue Action.

Christians, C. G. (2008). Between the summits: Media ethics theory, education and literature. In J. M. Kittross (Ed.), *An ethics trajectory: Visions of media past, present and yet to come* (pp. 29–53). Urbana, IL: University of Illinois/the Institute of Communications Research.

Cooper, T. W. (2009). *The quintessential Christians: Judging his books by their covers and leitmotifs.* Paper presented at the Association for Education in Journalism and Mass Communication, Boston. Council of Public Relations Firms (2009). Resources section. Retrieved February 6, 2010, from http://www.prfirms.org

Curtin, P. A., & Boynton, L. A. (2001). Ethics in public relations: Theory and practice. In R. L. Heath (Ed.), *Handbook of public relations* (pp. 411–422). Thousand Oaks, CA: Sage.

Cutlip, S. M. (1995). *Public relations history from the 17th century to the 20th century: The antecedents.* Hillsdale, NJ: Lawrence Erlbaum.

Cutlip, S., Center, A., & Broom, G. (2006). *Effective Public Relations* (9th ed.). Upper Saddle, NJ: Pearson Prentice Hall.

De George, R. T. (2006). *Business ethics* (6th ed.). Upper Saddle River, NJ: Pearson Prentice Hall.

Dewey, J. (1927). *The public and* its *problems.* Chicago: Swallow.

Dozier, D. A., & Broom, G. M. (1995). Evolution of the manager role in public relations practice. *Journal of Public Relations Research, 7,* 3–26.

Dozier, D. M., & Ehling, W. P. (1992). Evaluation of public relations programs: What the literature tells us about their effects. In J. E. Grunig (Ed.), *Excellence in public relations and communication management* (pp. 159–184). Hillsdale, NJ: Lawrence Erlbaum Associates.

Ehling, W. P., & Dozier, D. M. (1992). Public relations management and operations research. In J. E. Grunig (Ed.), *Excellence in public relations and communication management* (pp. 251–284). Hillsdale, NJ: Lawrence Erlbaum Associates.

Elliott, D. (2007). Getting Mill right. *Journal of Mass Media Ethics, 22,* 100–112.

Embassy of the United States in Tripoli, Libya. (n.d.). *About the Embassy: U.S. embassy greeting and history.* Retrieved February 6, 2010, from http://libya.usembassy.gov/history2.html

Entergy, Hurricanes Katrina and Rita Final Executive Summary Report. (2005, October 18).

Esman, M. (1972). The elements of institution building. In J. W. Eaton (Ed.), *Institution Building and Development* (pp. 19–40). Beverly Hills, CA: Sage.

Evan, W. (1976). An organization-set model of interorganizational relations. In W. Evan (Ed.), *Interorganizational Relations* (pp. 78–90). New York: Penguin.

Fitzpatrick, K., & Gauthier C. (2001). Toward a professional responsibility theory of public relations ethics. *Journal of Mass Media Ethics, 16,* 205.

Freeman, R. E. (1984). *Strategic management: A stakeholder approach.* Boston: Pitman.

Gass, R. H., & Seiter, J. S. (2009). Credibility and public diplomacy. In N. Snow & P. M. Taylor (Eds.), *Routledge handbook of public diplomacy* (pp. 154–165). New York: Routledge.

Goldberg, M. (Ed.). (1993). *Against the grain: New approaches to professional ethics.* Valley Forge, PA: Trinity Press International.

Goldman, R., Radia, K., & Berman, J. T. (2009, September 23). Mr. Gadhafi, tear down that tent: Moammar Gadhafi packs up his tent; won't stay in New York suburb. Retrieved February 6, 2010, from http://abcnews.go.com/International/Politics/gaddafis-tent-blocked-stop-work-order/story?id=8649084

Goodpaster, K. E. (2007). *Conscience and corporate culture.* Malden, MA: Blackwell.

Griffin, R. W. (2008). *Fundamentals of management* (5th ed.). Boston: Houghton Mifflin.

Grunig, J. E. (1984). Organizations, environments, and models of public relations. *Public Relations Research and Education, 1*(1), 6–29.

Grunig, J. E. (Ed.). (1992). *Excellence in public relations and communication management.* Hillsdale, NJ: Lawrence Erlbaum Associates.

Grunig, J. E. (2001). Two-way symmetrical public relations: Past, present, and future. In R. L. Heath (Ed.), *Handbook of public relations* (pp. 11–30). Thousand Oaks, CA: Sage.

Grunig, J. E. (2005). Situational theory of publics. In *Encyclopedia of public relations* (p. 779). Thousand Oaks, CA: Sage.

Grunig, J. E., & Grunig, L. A. (1992). Models of public relations and communications. In J. E. Grunig (Ed.), *Excellence in public relations and communication management* (pp. 285–326). Hillsdale, NJ: Lawrence Erlbaum Associates.

Grunig, J. E., Grunig L. A., & Ehling, W. P. (1992). What is an effective organization? In J. E. Grunig (Ed.), *Excellence in public relations and communication management* (pp. 65–90). Hillsdale, NJ: Lawrence Erlbaum Associates.

Grunig, J. E., & Hunt, T. (1984). *Managing public relations.* New York: Holt, Rinehart and Winston.

Grunig, J. E., & Repper, F. C. (1992). Strategic management, publics, and issues. In J. E. Grunig (Ed.), *Excellence in public relations and communication management* (pp. 117–157). Hillsdale, NJ: Lawrence Erlbaum Associates.

Grunig, L. A. (1992a). Activism: How it limits the effectiveness of organizations and how excellent public relations departments respond. In J. E. Grunig (Ed.), *Excellence in public relations and communication management* (pp. 503–530). Hillsdale, NJ: Lawrence Erlbaum Associates.

Grunig, L. A. (1992b). How public relations/communication departments should adapt to the structure and environment of an organization . . . and what they actually do. In J. E. Grunig (Ed.), *Excellence in public relations and communication management* (pp. 467–481). Hillsdale, NJ: Lawrence Erlbaum Associates.

Grunig, L. A., Grunig, J. E., & Dozier, D. M. (2002). *Excellent public relations and effective organizations: A study of communication management in three countries*. Mahwah, NJ: Lawrence Erlbaum Associates.

Grunig, L. A., Grunig, J. E., & Ehling, W. P. (1992). What is an effective organization? In J. E. Grunig (Ed.), *Excellence in public relations and communication management* (pp. 65–90). Hillsdale, NJ: Lawrence Erlbaum Associates.

Hambrick, D. C. (1981). Environment, strategy, and power within top management teams. *Administrative Science Quarterly, 26*, 253–276.

Hazleton, L. (2009, September 23). Have you got a permit for that Bedouin tent sir? Colonel Ghaddafi meets his match…New York planning officials. Retrieved February 6, 2010, from http://www.dailymail.co.uk/news/worldnews/article-1215509/Have-got-permit-Bedouin-tent-sir-Colonel-Gaddafi-meets-match—New-York-planning-officials.html

Heath, R. L. (1997). *Strategic issues management: Organizations and public policy challenges*. Thousand Oaks, CA: Sage.

Hendrix, J. A. (2000). *Public relations cases* (7th ed.). Belmont, CA: Wadsworth.

Hickson, M. L. (2003). Qualitative methodology. In J. E. Hocking, D. W. Stacks, & S. T. McDermott, *Communication research* (3rd ed., pp. 193–214). Boston: Allyn & Bacon.

Home Depot, Inc. (2009). The Value Wheel and The Inverted Pyramid. Personal communication. Taken from presentation made by Brad Shaw.

Hoover's Handbook of American Business. (1997). Austin, TX: Hoover's Business Press.

House OKs ban on horse slaughter for meat. (2009, September 7). *Associated Press*. Retrieved September 7, 2009, from http://www.foxnews.com/story/0,2933,212726,00.html

Halpern, M. (2006, May 16). *Bad boy turned big boy: Muammar Ghadaffi*. Retrieved February 6, 2010, from http://micahhalpern.com/archives/2006/05/bad_boy_turned.html

IEStormNet Update. Entergy New Orleans and city council agree to modest, phased-in rate plan. (2006, October 27).

Kant, I. (1785/1964). *Groundwork of the metaphysic of morals* (H. J. Paton, Trans.). New York: Harper & Row.

Kant, I. (1963). *Lectures on ethics* (L. Infield, Trans.). Indianapolis, IN: Hackett.

Katz, D., & Kahn, R. L. (1966). *The social psychology of organizations*. New York: John Wiley & Sons.

Kidder, R. M. (2005). *Moral courage: Taking action when your values are put to the test*. New York: HarperCollins.

Laszlo, E. (1996). *The systems view of the world: A holistic vision for our time*. Cresskill, NJ: Hampton Press.

Leeper, K. A. (1996). Public relations ethics and communitarinism: A preliminary investigation. *Public Relations Review, 22*, 163–179.

Lerbinger, O. (2006). *Corporate public affairs: Interacting with interest groups, media, and government.* Mahwah, NJ: Lawrence Erlbaum Associates.

Liechty, G. (1997). The limits of collaboration. *Public Relations Review, 23*, 48.

Lindenmann, W. K. (2003). *Guidelines for measuring the effectiveness of PR programs and activities.* Institute for Public Relations. Retrieved February 6, 2010, from http://www.instituteforpr.org/research_single/measuring_activities

Luhmann, N. (1984). *Social systems* (J. Bednarz & D. Baecker, Trans.). Stanford, CA: Stanford University Press.

Marston, J. E. (1979). *Modern public relations.* New York: McGraw-Hill.

Martinson, D. L. (1994). Enlightened self-interest fails as an ethical baseline in public relations. *Journal of Mass Media Ethics, 9*, 100–108.

Miles, M. B., & Huberman, A. M. (1994). *Qualitative data analysis: An expanded sourcebook* (2nd ed.). Thousand Oaks, CA: Sage.

Mintzberg, H. (1980). Structure in 5's: A synthesis of research on organization design. *Management Science, 26*, 322–341.

Mintzberg, H. (1983). *Power in and around organizations.* Englewood Cliffs, NJ: Prentice Hall.

Mitchell, R. K., Agle, B. R., & Wood, D. J. (1997). Toward a theory of stakeholder identification and salience: Defining the principle of who and what really counts. *Academy of Management Review, 22*, 853–886.

Murphy, P. (1991). The limits of symmetry: A game theory approach to symmetric and asymmetrical public relations. *Public Relations Research Annual, 3*, 115–131.

Murphy, P. E. (1998). *Eighty exemplary ethics statements.* Notre Dame, IN: University of Notre Dame Press.

Murphy, P., & Dee, J. (1992). DuPont and Greenpeace: The dynamics of conflict between corporations and activist groups. *Journal of Public Relations Research, 4*, 3–20.

Paine, K. D. (2007). *Measuring public relationships: The data-driven communicator's guide to success.* Berlin, NH: KDPaine & Partners.

Parks, S. D. (1993). Professional ethics, moral courage, and the limits of personal virtue. In B. Darling-Smith (Ed.), *Can virtue be taught?* Notre Dame, IN: University of Notre Dame Press.

Parsons, T. (1976). Three levels in the hierarchical structure of organizations. In W. Evan (Ed.), *Interorganizational Relations* (pp. 69–78). New York: Penguin.

Paton, H. J. (1967). *The categorical imperative: A study in Kant's moral philosophy.* New York: Harper & Row.

Pfeffer, J., & Salancik, G. R. (1978). *The external control of organizations: A resource dependence perspective*. New York: Harper & Row.

Public Relations Society of America. (2009a). *Official statement on public relations*. Retrieved February 6, 2010, from http://www.prsa.org/aboutprsa/publicrelationsdefined/Official Statement on Public Relations.pdf

Public Relations Society of America. (2009b). *Public relations defined*. Retrieved February 6, 2010, from http://www.prsa.org/aboutprsa/publicrelationsdefined

Qaddafi tent back up on Trump's N.Y. estate. (2009, September 24). *Associated Press*. Retrieved February 6, 2010, from http://www.foxnews.com/story/0,2933,555260,00.html

Rawlins, B. L. (2006). *Prioritizing stakeholders for public relations*. Institute for Public Relations. Retrieved February 6, 2010, from http://www.instituteforpr.org/research_single/prioritizing_stakeholders

Renfro, W. L. (1993). *Issues management in strategic planning*. Westport, CT: Quorum Books.

Robbins, S. P. (1990). *Organization theory: Structure, design, and applications* (3rd ed.). Englewood Cliffs, NJ: Prentice Hall.

Ross, W. D. (2002). *The right and the good*. Oxford: Clarendon Press.

Sage, A. (2007, November 24). Consternation as Muammar Ghaddafi seeks to pitch his tent on Nicolas Sarkozy's lawn. Retrieved February 6, 2010, from http://www.timesonline.co.uk/tol/news/world/europe/article2933205.ece#

Saunders, C. S. (1981). Management information systems, communications, and departmental power: An integrative model. *Academy of Management Review*, *6*, 431–442.

Seeger, M. W. (1997). *Ethics and organizational communication*. Cresskill, NJ: Hampton Press.

Sims, R. R. (1994). *Ethics and organizational decision making: A call for renewal*. Westport, CT: Quorum.

Sims, R. R., & Brinkman, J. (2003). Enron ethics (or, culture matters more than codes). *Journal of Business Ethics*, *45*, 243–256.

Singer, P. (1994). Introduction. In *Ethics* (pp. 3–13). Oxford: Oxford University Press.

Sriramesh, K. Grunig, J. E., & Buffington, J. (1992). Corporate culture and public relations. In J. E. Grunig (Ed.), *Excellence in public relations and communication management* (pp. 577–596). Hillsdale, NJ: Lawrence Erlbaum Associates.

Stacks, D. W. (2002). *Primer of public relations research*. New York: Guilford.

Stacks, D. W., & Michaelson, D. (2009). Exploring the comparative communications effectiveness of advertising and public relations: A replication and extension of prior experiments. *Public Relations Journal, 3*, 1–22.

Stacks, D. W., & Michaelson, D. (in press). *A practitioner's guide to public relations research, measurement and evaluation.* New York: Business Expert Press.

Stoffels, J. D. (1994). *Strategic issues management: A comprehensive guide to environmental scanning.* Milwaukee, WI: Pergamon.

Tashakkori, A., & Teddlie, C. (1998). *Mixed methodology: Combining qualitative and quantitative approaches.* Thousand Oaks, CA: Sage.

United States v. National City Lines, Inc., et al. United States Court of Appeals for the Seventh Circuit, 186 F.2d 562.

Vercic, D., Grunig, L. A., & Grunig, J. E. (1996). Global and specific principles of public relations: Evidence from Slovenia. In H. M. Culbertson & N. Chen (Eds.), *International public relations: A comparative analysis* (pp. 31–65). Mahwah, NJ: Lawrence Erlbaum Associates.

Waters, J. A., & Bird, F. (1987). The moral dimension of organizational culture. *Journal of Business Ethics, 6*, 15–22.

Weick, K. E. (1969). *The social psychology of organizing.* Reading, MA: Addison-Wesley.

Wilson, L. (2005). *Strategic program planning for effective public relations campaigns.* Dubuque, IA: Kendall/Hunt.

Winn, M. I. (2001). Building stakeholder theory with a decision modeling methodology. *Business & Society, 40*, 133–166.

Wordsworth, A. (2009, August 31). Colonel Ghadaffi's tent ruffles feathers in New Jersey. Retrieved February 6, 2010, from http://network.nationalpost.com/np/blogs/fullcomment/archive/2009/08/31/col-gaddafi-s-tent-diplomacy-ruffles-feathers-in-new-jersey.aspx#

Wright, D. K. (1985). Can age predict the moral values of public relations practitioners? *Public Relations Review, 11*, 51–60.

Yin, R. K. (1994). *Case study research: Design and methods* (2nd ed.). Thousand Oaks, CA: Sage.

Index

Note: Page numbers in italics refer to figures and tables.

D

E

F

G

H

I

J

K

L

M

P

Q

R

S

T

U

V

W